FAITH LESSONS
ON THE
ministry life &
of the
Messiah

PARTICIPANT'S GUIDE

Also Available from Ray Vander Laan

Video and Group Resources

Faith Lessons on the Death and Resurrection of the Messiah
Faith Lessons on the Promised Land
Faith Lessons on the Prophets and Kings of Israel

Book and Audiocassette

Echoes of His Presence

CD-Rom

Jesus: An Interactive Journey

FAITH LESSONS
ON THE life &
ministry of the
THE
Messiah

PARTICIPANT'S GUIDE

Ray Vander Laan

with
Stephen and Amanda Sorenson

ZONDERVAN™

GRAND RAPIDS, MICHIGAN 49530

ZONDERVAN™

Faith Lessons on the Life and Ministry of the Messiah Participant's Guide
Copyright © 1999 by Ray Vander Laan

Requests for information should be addressed to:

Zondervan, *Grand Rapids, Michigan 49530*

ISBN 0-310-67898-6

Interior design by Sherri Hoffman

Printed in the United States of America

06 /❖DC/ 20 19 18 17

contents

introduction

Because God speaks to us through the Scriptures, studying them is a rewarding experience. The inspired human authors of the Bible, as well as those to whom the words were originally given, were primarily Jews living in the Near East. God's words and actions spoke to them with such power, clarity, and purpose that they wrote them down and carefully preserved them as an authoritative body of literature.

God's use of human servants in revealing Himself resulted in writings that clearly bear the stamp of time and place. The message of the Scriptures is, of course, eternal and unchanging—but the circumstances and conditions of the people of the Bible are unique to their times. Consequently, we most clearly understand God's truth when we know the cultural context within which He spoke and acted and the perception of the people with whom He communicated. This does not mean that God's revelation is unclear if we don't know the cultural context. Rather, by learning how to think and approach life as Abraham, Moses, Ruth, Esther, and Paul did, modern Christians will deepen their appreciation of God's Word. To fully apply the message of the Bible, we must enter the world of the Hebrews and familiarize ourselves with their culture.

That is the purpose of this study. The events and characters of the Bible are presented in their original settings. Although the videos offer the latest archaeological research, this series is not intended to be a definitive cultural and geographical study of the lands of the Bible. No original scientific discoveries are revealed here. The purpose of this study is to help us better understand God's revealed mission for our lives by enabling us to hear and see His words in their original context.

understanding the world of the Hebrews

More than 3,800 years ago, God spoke to His servant Abraham: "Go, walk through the length and breadth of the land, for I am giving it to you" (Genesis 13:17). From the outset, God's choice of a Hebrew nomad to begin His plan of salvation (that is still unfolding) was linked to the selection of a specific land where His redemptive work would begin. The nature of God's covenant relationship with His people demanded a place where their faith could be exercised and displayed to all nations so that the world would know of *Yahweh,* the true and faithful God. God showed the same care in preparing a land for His chosen people as He did in preparing a people to live in that land. For us to fully understand God's plan and purpose for His people, we must first understand the nature of the place He selected for them.

By New Testament times, the Jewish people had been removed from the Promised Land by the Babylonians due to Israel's failure to live obediently before God (Jeremiah 25:4–11). The exile lasted seventy years, but its impact upon God's people was astounding. New patterns of worship developed, and scribes and experts in God's law shaped the new commitment to be faithful to Him. The prophets predicted the appearance of a Messiah like King David who would revive the kingdom of the Hebrew people.

But the Promised Land was now home to many other groups of people whose religious practices, moral values, and lifestyles conflicted with those of the Jews. Living as God's witnesses took on added difficulty as Greek, Roman, and Samaritan worldviews mingled with that of the Israelites. The Promised Land was divided between kings and governors, usually under the authority of one foreign empire or another. But the mission of God's people did not change. They were still to live *so that the world would know that their God was the true God.* And the land continued to provide them opportunity to encounter the world that desperately needed to know this reality.

The Promised Land was the arena within which God's people were to serve Him faithfully as the world watched. The land God chose for His people was on the crossroads of the world. A major trade route, the Via Maris, ran through it. God intended for the Israelites to take control of the cities along this route and thereby exert influence on the nations around them. Through their righteous living, the Hebrews were to reveal the one true God, *Yahweh,* to the world. They failed to accomplish this mission, however, because of their unfaithfulness.

Western Christianity tends to spiritualize the concept of the Promised Land as it is presented in the Bible. Instead of seeing it as a crossroads from which to influence the world, modern Christians view it as a distant, heavenly city, a glorious "Canaan" toward which we are traveling as we ignore the world around us. We are focused on the destination, not the journey. We have unconsciously separated our walk with God from our responsibility to the world in which He has placed us. In one sense, our earthly experience is simply preparation for an eternity in the "promised land." Preoccupation with this idea, however, distorts the mission God has set for us.

Living by faith is not a vague, otherworldly experience; rather, it is being faithful to God right now, in the place and time in which He has put us. This truth is emphasized by God's choice of Canaan, a crossroads of the ancient world, as the Promised Land for the Israelites. God wants His people to be in the game, not on the bench. Our mission, as Christians today, is the same one He gave to the Israelites. We are to live obediently *within* the world so that through us *the world may know that our God is the one true God.*

The Assumptions of Biblical Writers

Biblical writers assumed that their readers were familiar with Near Eastern geography. The geography of Canaan shaped the culture of the people living there. Their settlements began near sources of water and food. Climate and raw materials shaped their choice of occupation, dress, weapons, diet, and even artistic expression. As their cities grew, they interacted politically. Trade developed, and trade routes were established.

During New Testament times, the Promised Land was called Palestine or Judea. *Judea* (which means "Jewish") technically referred to the land that had been the nation of Judah. Because of the influence that the people of Judea had over the rest of the land, the land itself was called Judea. The Romans divided the land into several provinces, including Judea, Samaria, and Galilee (the three main divisions during Jesus' time); Gaulanitis, the Decapolis, and Perea (east of the Jordan River); and Idumaea (Edom) and Nabatea (in the south). These further divisions of Israel added to the rich historical and cultural background God prepared for the coming of Jesus and the beginning of His church.

Today the names *Israel* and *Palestine* are often used to designate the land God gave to Abraham. Both terms are politically charged. *Palestine* is used by the Arabs living in the central part of the country, while *Israel* is used by the Jews to indicate the State of Israel. In this study,

Israel is used in the biblical sense. This choice does not indicate a political statement regarding the current struggle in the Middle East but instead is chosen to best reflect the biblical designation for the land.

Unfortunately, many Christians do not have even a basic geographical knowledge of the region. This series is designed to help solve that problem. We will be studying the people and events of the Bible in their geographical and historical contexts. Once we know the *who*, *what*, and *where* of a Bible story, we will be able to understand the *why*. By deepening our understanding of God's Word, we can strengthen our relationship with God.

The biblical writers also used a language that, like all languages, is bound by culture and time. Therefore, understanding the Scriptures involves more than knowing what the words mean. We need to also understand those words from the perspective of the people who used them.

The people whom God chose as His instruments—the people to whom He revealed Himself—were Hebrews living in the Near East. These people described their world and themselves in concrete terms. Their language was one of pictures, metaphors, and examples rather than ideas, definitions, and abstractions. Whereas we might describe God as omniscient or omnipresent (knowing everything and present everywhere), a Hebrew would have preferred to describe God by saying, "The Lord is my shepherd." Thus, the Bible is filled with concrete images from Hebrew culture: God is our Father, and we are His children; God is the potter, and we are the clay; Jesus is the Lamb killed on Passover; heaven is an oasis in the desert, and hell is the city sewage dump; the Last Judgment will be in the Eastern Gate of the heavenly Jerusalem and will include sheep and goats.

These people had an Eastern mind-set rather than a Western mindset. Eastern thought emphasizes the process of learning as much or more than the end result. Whereas Westerners tend to collect information to find the right answer, Hebrew thought stresses the process of discovery as well as the answer. So as you go through this study, use it as an opportunity to deepen your understanding of who God is and to grow in your relationship with Him.

In the shadow of Herod

Questions to think about

1. Think of some instances in the Bible when that which appeared to be weak and powerless defeated that which appeared to be stronger and more powerful. What thoughts and feelings do these instances bring to mind?

2. What do you think are the most powerful, undefeatable evidences of evil in our world today?

3. Do you agree or disagree with the statement: "It doesn't seem as though God can do much about evil." Explain your view.

video notes

The Herodion in Its Setting

Israel and Edom, a History of Conflict

Herod the Edomite Versus Jesus the King of Kings

video Highlights

1. Which details about the Herodion made the greatest impression on you?

2. What is significant about the Herodion's proximity to Bethlehem?

3. What are some of the contrasts highlighted between King Herod and Jesus?

4. How do the birth of the twins, Jacob and Esau, and Balaam's prophecy relate to Jesus and Herod?

5. How has this video changed your view of the step of faith that was required for the Jews to believe that Jesus was the Messiah?

PROFILE OF A FORTRESS

The Awesome Herodion

- Built about thirty years before Jesus' birth on a hilltop at the edge of the Judea Wilderness to provide an escape for Herod in the event of danger in Jerusalem.
- Rose more than forty-five feet above the hilltop and could be seen from as far as ten miles away in Jerusalem.
- Located near the site of Herod's battlefield victory over the Hasmonaeans, which earned him the Roman nomination to be the earthly king of the Jews.

The Herodion: A Mountaintop Fortress

- Overshadowed Bethlehem, about three miles away, where Jesus, the almighty King, was born.
- Was often passed by shepherds (such as those who came to see the baby Jesus) and farmers who lived in Bethlehem—a small town of at most several hundred people. Bethlehem had fertile farmland and was also close to the wilderness where flocks were kept.

The Upper Palace

The Herodion

- Had double cylindrical walls about fifteen feet apart with an outside diameter of nearly 220 feet. Between the walls were seven stories of apartments, chambers, and storage rooms. Herod covered the lower four stories with packed dirt, creating the unique, volcanic-cone shape.

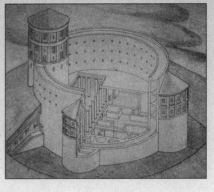

- Was protected by smaller defensive towers on the south, north, and west that extended outside the cylindrical structure. The enormous eastern tower was 55 feet in diameter, more than 120 feet tall, and provided royal apartments for King Herod and his family.

Inside the Herodion

- Contained a glorious bath complex that included a vaulted caldarium (hot bath), tepidarium (warm bath), and frigidarium (cold bath)—each of which had floors decorated with mosaics. Herod brought water from more than three miles away through aqueducts and stored it in cisterns at the base of the fortress-palace.
- Could accommodate many guests in its large, roofed reception hall that had colored plaster walls. During the Jewish revolts long after Herod's death, the Zealots made this hall into a synagogue.
- Had an open-air garden with columns on three sides and a niche at each end for statues.
- Was entered by a three-hundred-step stairway on the outside of the mountain followed by a two-hundred-foot tunnel that led into the fortress.

The Lower Palace

- Consisted of a complex of buildings and a pool at the foot of the mountain. The pool—one of the largest in the ancient world—was 10 feet deep, 140 feet long, 200 feet wide, and was surrounded by colonnaded gardens—quite a sight given that the water came via aqueduct from more than three miles away. In the middle of the pool was an island more than forty feet in diameter containing a colonnaded circular building in which Herod and guests could relax in complete privacy.
- Contained a huge building complex between the pool and the upper fortress, with more than 400 feet of elaborate halls and guest rooms. In front was a terrace more than 1,000 feet long.

(continued on page 16)

(continued from page 15)

- Presumably holds the tomb of Herod. However, this largest of the fortress structures has not yet been completely excavated.

The Herodion: Lower Palace

small Group Bible Discovery

Topic A: Bethlehem—Small But Significant

Despite its small size, Bethlehem was the location of significant historical events. Discovering its history helps us to appreciate why the town was the perfect place for Jesus' birth.

1. Look at the map of Israel below. Note Bethlehem's location in relationship to Jerusalem, the Herodion, the Judea Wilderness, the Judea Mountains, Moab, and Edom (Idumaea). Which occupations did Bethlehem's unique location at the border between the mountains and the wilderness enable its people to have?

Topography of Israel: New Testament

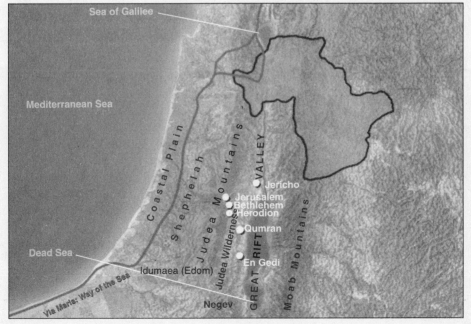

2. Where was Jacob traveling to when Rachel died in child-birth? (See Genesis 35:16–19.)

3. What do King David and Ruth, who are mentioned in the following verses, have in common? (See Ruth 1:22; 1 Samuel 16:1–3; Matthew 1:1, 5.)

4. What does Scripture reveal about Moab, the country in which Ruth was reared? (See Genesis 19:36–37; Numbers 24:17; 1 Kings 11:7; 2 Kings 3:26–27.) What does the fact that God blessed the entire world through Ruth reveal about how God uses people in His plan of salvation?

5. What did Micah predict about seven hundred years before Jesus was born? (See Micah 5:2.)

6. Why was it important for Jesus to be born in Bethlehem?
    (See Matthew 1:1, 17; Luke 1:29–33; 2:4–7.)

DID YOU KNOW?

Worlds Apart, But Still Within View

East of the Dead Sea, which is barely ten miles from Bethlehem, are the mountains of Moab where Ruth was reared. Thus, when Ruth moved to Bethlehem with Naomi, she probably moved fewer than twenty miles. She could even see her homeland on a clear day. What a significant, but not extensive, trip that turned out to be!

The Wilderness East of Bethlehem

Topic B: God's Plan for the Birth of the Savior Unfolds

1. Read the following verses and note what you discover
    about the individuals involved and the way in which God
    used them to bring about the birth of Jesus.

    a. Genesis 38:6–19, 24–26; Matthew 1:1, 3a

    b. Joshua 2:1–11, 6:22–25; Matthew 1:1, 5a

    c. Ruth 1:1–6, 15–18; 4:9–17; 1 Kings 11:7; 2 Kings
        3:26–27; Matthew 1:1, 5b

    d. 1 Samuel 16:1–13; Matthew 1:1, 6

   e. 2 Samuel 11:1–5, 14–17, 26–27; 12:13–25; Matthew
      1:1, 6b

2. What do the above passages reveal about God's choice of
     people who participated in His plan of salvation—to be in
     Jesus' ancestral line?

3. Of all the other people God could have chosen, why do
     you think He selected these people to have a role in help-
     ing to accomplish the birth of Messiah the King?

KEY DATES

586 B.C.	Babylonian captivity of Judah
538 B.C.	Return to Israel
332 B.C.	Alexander the Great conquers Israel
330–198 B.C.	Rule of Hellenistic Ptolemies over the Jews
198–167 B.C.	Oppression under Hellenistic Seleucids
167 B.C.	Maccabee revolt
167–63 B.C.	Hasmonaean kingdom
37 B.C.	Herod the Great begins his reign
4 B.C.	Herod the Great dies
ca. 6 B.C.	Jesus' birth
ca. A.D. 30	Jesus is crucified
A.D. 70	Roman destruction of Jerusalem during First Jewish Revolt
A.D. 131–135	Bar Kochba Revolt (Second Jewish Revolt)

Topic C: A Contrast Between Two Kings

1. Read Matthew 2:1–8, 16–18.

   a. Based on the video and your reading, what do you think motivated Herod the Great?

   b. In what way(s) did King Herod respond to his potential rivals, specifically to Jesus?

2. What motivated Jesus—the Messiah, the King of the universe—to do what He did on earth? (See John 4:34; 5:30; 8:54; 10:10, 17.)

3. Describe the contrasts between Jesus and Herod that can be found "beneath the surface" of Matthew 2:1.

4. Given the differences between King Herod and the infant Messiah, why was the shepherds' visit to Bethlehem such an act of faith? (See Luke 2:8–18.)

5. Describe how the wise men exercised their faith after speaking with Herod and continuing on to Bethlehem (with the great Herodion clearly in view) to find the baby Jesus. (See Matthew 2:1–12.)

6. By bringing Jesus and King Herod—two kings who couldn't have been more different—together at the same time in history, what was God revealing about how He works?

PROFILES IN CONTRAST

Jesus	Herod the Great
Placed in a manger	Lived in magnificent palaces
Appeared as a weak and powerless baby	Appeared to have great strength and power
Had no earthly status but really had it all—eternal power, glory, authority, etc.	Had great earthly status, but lacked eternal status
Lived to honor His Father	Lived to glorify himself
Used by God to fulfill the purposes of God	Lived to fulfill his own purposes
Built a kingdom of people (Matthew 16:18; 1 Peter 2:4–8)	Built glorious buildings of marble and other stones
Built for the glory of God so others would know Yahweh is truly God	Built to honor himself and maintain good relations with Rome
Dedicated to serving others	Was self-serving
Had ultimate authority and still does (Ephesians 1:18–22)	Had only limited earthly authority
Died in agony on the cross to remove the sins of humankind	Died in agony, hated by his family, after ordering one of his sons to be executed
The Messiah from Jacob's lineage who overcame all evil but was never accepted as King of the Jews	The Edomite whose reign violated God's rules (Deuteronomy 17:15) and was never accepted by the Jews

Topic D: Israel and Edom, Nations in Conflict

1. What does Genesis 25:21–26 reveal about Jacob and Esau, the grandsons of Abraham?

2. Who were the descendants of Esau? (See Genesis 25:29–30; 36:1–9.)

3. What did Balaam prophesy would happen to Jacob's people—Israel—and to Esau's people—the Edomites? (See Numbers 24:15–19.)

4. What characterized the history of relationships between Israel and Edom? (See Numbers 20:18–21; 1 Kings 11:14–17; 2 Kings 8:20–22; Ezekiel 25:12–14.)

5. What did Obadiah and other prophets predict would happen to the descendants of Jacob and Esau? (See Jeremiah
   49:8–10; Ezekiel 35:15; Amos 1:11–12; 9:11–12; Obadiah
   8–14, 18.)

6. History reveals that Herod the Great came from Idumaea,
   which was Edom. How does what Jesus accomplished on
   earth during Herod's reign fit with the prophecies about
   Israel and Edom?

faith Lesson

Time for Reflection

Read the following passage of Scripture and take the next few minutes to reflect on the great step of faith that was required for the Jews of Jesus' day to believe that He was the Messiah.

And there were shepherds living out in the fields nearby, keeping watch over their flocks at night. An angel of the Lord appeared to them, and the glory of the Lord shone around them, and they were terrified. But the angel said to them, "Do not be afraid. I bring you good news of great joy that will be for all the people. Today in the town of David a Savior has been born to you; he is Christ the Lord. This will be a sign to you: You will find a baby wrapped in cloths and lying in a manger."

Suddenly a great company of the heavenly host appeared with the angel, praising God and saying,

"Glory to God in the highest,
and on earth peace to men on
whom his favor rests."

When the angels had left them and gone into heaven, the shepherds said to one another, "Let's go to Bethlehem and see this thing that has happened, which the Lord has told us about."

So they hurried off and found Mary and Joseph, and the baby, who was lying in the manger. When they had seen him, they spread the word concerning what had been told them about this child, and all who heard it were amazed at what the shepherds said to them. But Mary treasured up all these things and pondered them in her heart. The shepherds returned, glorifying and praising God for all the things they had heard and seen, which were just as they had been told.

LUKE 2:8–20

1. Think about what a step of faith it was for the shepherds to respond as they did to the news of the Messiah's birth.

   a. What earthly king would send such an important announcement to mere shepherds?

   b. What would Herod have done to the shepherds if he had discovered they had actually visited and worshiped another king?

   c. Why would it have been frightening for these events to occur, as they did, in plain view of the Herodion?

   d. Why was it a great risk to tell others what had happened—that a new king, the King of heaven and earth, had been born?

2. If you had been a bystander when Jesus was born, who would you have believed was more powerful and worthy of your honor and allegiance—Jesus or King Herod? Why?

3. How is the commitment to Jesus you are asked to make similar to the one that people during His lifetime on earth were asked to make?

4. How does your commitment to Jesus as Messiah affect the way you relate to the "Herods" (evils) in your daily life?

Action Points

Take a moment to review the key points you explored today, then jot down an action step (or steps) that you will commit to this week as a result of what you have learned.

1. *It took great faith for the Jewish people to believe that Jesus, who began His life on earth as a baby in Bethlehem, was truly the Lord of heaven and earth.*

    The contrasts between Jesus and Herod could not have been greater. Herod had all the power, wealth, strength, and glory that his position in the world could offer, yet Jesus, the King of the universe, had nothing of that sort to demonstrate His position. So to believe in Jesus as the Messiah was to believe that regardless of outward appearances, Jesus, the baby in the manger, was indeed Lord of heaven and earth.

Today, Christians are asked to walk by faith, confident in the knowledge that things are not always as they appear to be, that God can use the weak to defeat the powerful. In what ways are you demonstrating faith in your walk with God? In what ways are you paying more attention to outward appearances rather than demonstrating faith in God?

2. *King Herod, who personified evil, no doubt seemed to have all the power and control. He ruled with an iron hand, seeking out and destroying every possible enemy—even killing innocent babies. Yet Jesus, the humble King of all creation, was truly in control. He had the power to overcome every evil—including that of Herod.*

Today, Christians are asked to believe that no matter how powerful Wall Street appears to be, no matter how controlling a government seems, no matter how influential the morals of Hollywood appear to be, no matter how evil pornography seems, no matter how overwhelming hunger, racism, or AIDS appear to be—Jesus Christ is King. Because His power, which has conquered all evil, resides within us, we do not need to fear the evil we face.

Although it is easier and safer to avoid evil than to confront it, the crucial question that all Christians must answer for themselves is: "Will I dare to live as if God is greater than any evil I face in my life and my culture, as if the power within me is greater than every power of evil that I will encounter?"

What or who are the "Herods" of your life today—the powers of evil that seem so strong and glorious or that seem more attractive and important than following Jesus?

Which opportunities has God given you to confront the power of the sinful world around you, based on the confidence that He—not Satan—is in control?

I believe that God is greater than any evil I will face, so I will dare to:

_____

_____

_____

_____

DATA FILE

The Works of a Master Builder

Herod the Great's visionary building programs, ingenious development of trade with other countries, and advancement of his nation's interests are remarkable. He used his magnificent building projects as part of his effort to strengthen his relationship with Rome and establish himself as the greatest king the Jews ever had.

The Temple Mount: A.D. 70

1 Temple	6 Double Gates	11 Barclay's Gate
2 Royal Stoa	7 Triple Gates	12 Wilson's Arch
3 Solomon's Colonnade	8 Ritual Baths	13 Warren's Gate
4 Southern Stairs	9 Plaza	14 Place of Trumpeting
5 South Wall	10 Robinson's Arch	15 Tyropoeon Street

Jerusalem

Herod rebuilt the temple out of marble and gold. The building was taller than a fifteen-story building, and its foundation included limestone blocks weighing more than five hundred tons. On the western hill of the city he built a spectacular palace complex that contained reception halls, apartments, fountains, gardens, baths, and a fortress for his personal guards. He also built a Greek theater and hippodrome, paved the streets, and installed sewers.

Masada

Perched atop a plateau in the Judea Wilderness, this fortress was one of the wonders of the ancient world. A spectacular palace suspended from one end of the plateau, luxurious hot and cold baths, mosaic floors, swimming pools, huge storehouses, barracks for soldiers, and cisterns holding millions of gallons of water helped to make this hot, dry wilderness outpost bearable for its occupants.

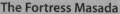

The Fortress Masada

Jericho

This palace was built on both sides of a wadi (a dry, deep riverbed), and a bridge spanned the riverbed. One wing contained a huge, marble-floored hall where Herod received guests. Next to it were peristyle gardens, dining halls, and a complete Roman bath. Across the wadi, another large building housed baths, a swimming pool, and gardens.

Caesarea

Needing contact with the Roman world for its military support and trade opportunities, Herod built Caesarea into one of the most amazing seaports of the ancient world. Founded in 22 B.C., the city housed a large theater, amphitheater, hippodrome, a massive temple to Augustus, and—

(continued on page 34)

(continued from page 33)

of course—an elaborate seaside palace. Much of the city was built with imported marble, and the city even had an elaborate sewer system that was cleansed by the sea.

The city's real glory, however, lay in its forty-acre, man-made harbor. A lighthouse guided ships into the harbor that brought Roman legions, marble, granite, and the Hellenistic culture into the region. From that harbor, ships also carried spices, olive oil, grain, and—most important—the gospel to the far reaches of the world.

Caesarea

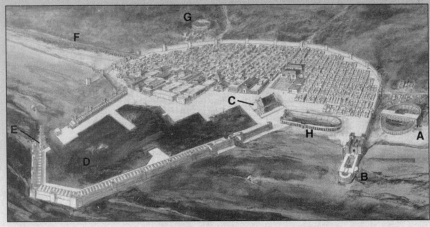

A Theater D Harbor (Sebastos) G Amphitheater
B Palace E Lighthouse H Hippodrome
C Temple of Augustus F Aqueduct

My Rock and My Fortress

Questions to Think About

1. Which images come to mind when you hear the word *fortress?*

2. When times get tough, when you face trouble or difficult times, what do you view as your personal "fortress"? What provides feelings of safety or security for you?

3. In what ways might God be considered our "fortress"?

video notes

Wilderness Fortresses

David's Masada

Herod's Masada

The Zealots' Masada

The Zealots' Commitment—More Than Words

video нighlights

1. Now that you have seen a bit of the Judea Wilderness, what do you think it was like for David and his men to hide out in the wilderness? What dangers and hazards, safety and hope did the wilderness offer?

2. In what ways would the type of wilderness experience David had encourage you to depend on God as your fortress? In what ways would it tempt you to depend upon yourself?

3. Which physical details about Masada surprised you?

4. What do you think about the Zealots' belief that it is wrong to owe allegiance to anyone or anything but God? What do you think about the way they carried out that belief?

small Group Bible Discovery

Topic A: A Fortress in the Wilderness

1. According to 1 Samuel 23:14, 24–29, where did David hide when King Saul was seeking to kill him? (On the map on page 39, locate the area described.)

2. Although David found safe hiding places in the wilderness, what, according to the following passages, did he consider to be his true protection?

    a. Psalm 18:1–2

    b. Psalm 18:46–50

Topography of Israel: New Testament

The Judea Wilderness

Jericho

Dead Sea

Qumran

En Gedi

Masada

Judea Mountains

Judea Wilderness

Jerusalem

Bethlehem

Moab Mountains

Jericho

Jerusalem
Bethlehem
Herodion

Qumran

VALLEY

GREAT RIFT

En Gedi

Judea Mountains

Judea Wilderness

Shephelah

Negev

Idumaea (Edom)

Sea of Galilee

Mediterranean Sea

Coastal Plain

Dead Sea

Via Maris: Way of the Sea

c. Psalm 63:1

Living Water Brings Life

d. Psalm 71:1–3

e. Psalm 144:2

3. Long after David sought refuge from King Saul, Herod the Great built the fortress of Masada in the same wilderness. In what ways did David and Herod view their protection differently?

4. With the contrasting views of Herod and David fresh in mind, read Matthew 6:25–34 and consider how Jesus would have you view your efforts to protect and provide for your needs.

DATA FILE

The Glories of Masada

Why Masada?

Herod built the fortress-palace of Masada on a huge rock plateau over-looking the Dead Sea in the barren, remote Judea Wilderness. The top of the plateau, more than twenty-one acres in size, is nearly 1,300 feet above the sea. Obviously Masada's height provided its greatest protection. But Herod also surrounded the summit with a wall and thirty defensive tow-ers. The fortress could be reached only via the Snake Path, the main, twist-ing path on the eastern side of the mountain, and a path on the western side. Strong, heavily guarded gates protected each of these entrances into the fortress.   (continued on page 42)

Masada

1. The Mountain
2. Northern Palace
3. Western Palace
4. Roman Bathhouse
5. Cistern
6. Storehouse

(continued from page 41)

Although located in a desert wilderness, Masada was close to more hospitable areas. Herod could quickly leave Jerusalem and flee to Masada if the Jewish people revolted or if Herod's Roman master, Antony, gave Herod's domain to Cleopatra, his enemy to the south. Masada was also near the southern areas of Nabatea and Idumaea, the countries of Herod's origin.

Masada's Palaces

Built into the northern end of the mountain was a remarkable building known as the "hanging palace." The upper level perched on top of the mountain, and the two lower levels were built into the cliff face.

• The upper terrace featured lavish living quarters with mosaic floors, frescoed walls, and a semicircular balcony that offered spectacular views.

Masada: Northern Palace

Column

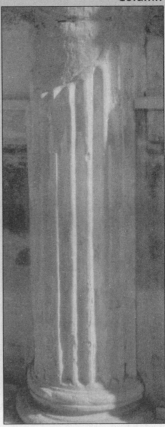

Mosaic

- The round, middle terrace had two concentric rows of columns that created a beautiful balcony for relaxation.
- The lower terrace, surrounded by low walls and columns with a roof in between, provided an open court inside a colonnade. A bathroom on its eastern side had mosaic floors. The great retaining walls that supported this level remain a testimony to the genius of Herod's engineers.

The western palace served as Herod's main living quarters in Masada. Occupying more than 37,000 square feet, this building included royal apartments, bathrooms, a cold-water pool, and a large reception hall with magnificently decorated mosaic pavement. Nearby were servants' quarters, workshops, a huge kitchen, and three richly decorated palaces—probably for the families of Herod's wives, who did not get along.

Water: Masada's Greatest Luxury

Despite its dry, wilderness location, Masada boasted one of the largest bathing complexes of its time. The largest room of the Roman bathhouse contained a hot bath (caldarium), which was much like a sauna. A warm bath (tepidarium) and cold bath (frigidarium) were adjacent. All of them were elegantly decorated with frescoes and mosaic floors. In addition, there were several swimming pools within the fortress.

To gather the water needed to supply such luxuries in the dry wilderness, Herod and his engineers created a brilliant water system that defied nature. Masada was perched on a mountain between two wadis that occasionally flooded when it rained in the mountains to the west. So Herod diverted some of the floodwater into twelve cisterns cut into the base of the mountain that could hold more than 1,500,000 cubic feet of water—enough water to sustain thousands of people for up to ten years! Water was bucketed up about three hundred feet and stored in large cisterns (perhaps old quarries for building stones) that could hold more than one million gallons on top of the plateau. Thus Masada had an enormous supply of fresh water. The elaborate bathing complexes and water supply reveal much about Herod's obsessive fears concerning safety and his craving for opulence and luxury.

(continued on page 44)

(continued from page 43)

Masada's Storehouses

Fifteen storehouses at Masada contained food, weapons, and other goods needed to provide security and luxury for Herod and his army. Some storerooms were filled with rows upon rows of amphorae (large pottery jars) in which olive oil, flour, wine, and other provisions were stored. Some storerooms were more than sixty feet long and twelve feet wide.

Storehouses of Masada

Topic B: The Quest for Their Own King

1. What did the Jews of Jesus' day eagerly await? Why did they want it so much? (See John 6:14–15.)

2. How did the desire of the Jewish people in general compare to the desire of the Zealots who captured and defended Masada?

3. What kind of freedom, peace, and kingdom did Jesus come
    to offer? (See John 8:31–32; 14:19–27; 16:33; 18:33–37.)

4. What do Matthew 10:2–4 and Acts 1:13 reveal about
    Simon, one of Jesus' disciples?

5. Consider the events that took place in Gethsemane when
    Jesus was arrested. In each of the following passages of Scrip-
    ture, what evidence do you see of the disciples' expectations
    for their Messiah? In contrast, what did Jesus have in mind?

The Gospel Account	The Disciples' Perception of God's Kingdom	The Kingdom of God as Jesus Knew It
Matthew 26:50–56		
Luke 22:47–52		
John 18:10–11		

6. What caused Jesus such deep grief as He approached Jerusalem on what we call "Palm Sunday" to the cheers of the people? (See Luke 19:35–44.)

7. After Jesus' resurrection, what did His disciples ask Him? What does their question reveal? (See Acts 1:1–6.)

TIMELINE OF EVENTS

198–167 B.C.	Oppression under Hellenistic Seleucids
167 B.C.	Maccabee revolt
167–63 B.C.	Hasmonaean kingdom
37 B.C.	Herod the Great begins his reign
ca. 6 B.C.	Jesus is born
4. B.C.	Herod the Great dies
ca. A.D. 30	Jesus is crucified
A.D. 66–73	First Jewish Revolt
A.D. 70	Jerusalem and the temple are destroyed
A.D. 73	Masada falls

WORTH OBSERVING

Jesus and the Jewish Revolts

Although Jesus was crucified by the Romans nearly forty years before the First Jewish Revolt, He understood the decision the Jewish people had to make concerning their Messiah. At least one of His disciples, Simon, was a Zealot (Matthew 10:4). His kingdom was not the kingdom of the Zealot or the sword, however (Matthew 26:51–52). Recognizing His people's patriotism, anger against the Romans, and desire for freedom, Jesus didn't trumpet His power. In fact, aware that many false messiahs were proclaiming messages, Jesus frequently commanded the people He taught and/or healed not to tell anyone what He had done for them—possibly because people might misunderstand His role in light of the growing nationalistic climate. (See Matthew 8:1–4; 9:27–30; 12:15–16; Luke 8:51–56; Mark 1:40–44; 3:10–12; 5:38–43; 7:33–36.) Even so, people often saw in Jesus a Davidic king, a military conqueror who would rescue them from the Romans (John 6:14–15; Acts 1:1–6).

Clearly, Jesus predicted the destruction that would result from the revolt (Matthew 24:1–2). His knowledge led Him to weep as He described what would happen (Luke 19:41–44). Some of His fellow Jews were looking for military solutions to their problems rather than spiritual ones, to a political messiah rather than the Lamb of God who came to take away the sins of the world. Jesus warned His followers not to participate in that method of bringing in God's kingdom. Whereas some Jewish people were seeking salvation through political and military might (which led to their future destruction), Jesus lived out and taught completely different truths.

Today, the Jewish people have returned to the land they lost in the First and Second Jewish Revolts, when some Jews sought God in the wrong places and in the wrong ways. Yet, the message of Jesus the Messiah remains unique and relevant, and we must be devoted to it. He alone is God's hope of peace (Luke 2:14).

A WORD OF CAUTION

Although many people of Jesus' day believed Him to be the Messiah, some still wanted to make Him into a military-political Messiah who would bring about freedom from Rome. Instead of listening to what and whom Jesus claimed to be, however, some people tried to make Him something else—and missed the peace and salvation He offered.

Today, the same thing is still happening. Many people try to make Jesus into someone other than who He is. (They declare Him to be a good man, for example, but vehemently deny His deity.) The ruins of Masada serve as poignant reminders of the strength and security that God our Fortress provides to His children, and also of what can happen when people misunderstand the gospel of Jesus.

Topic C: David: Committed to God, Even in the Wilderness

Recalling David's time in the desert wilderness near Masada and En Gedi provides important lessons for us in learning to trust God and depend on Him, particularly during times of trouble. David's faith in God and his willingness to submit to God's will have become a model to believers today.

1. Why did God reject Saul as king and select David? (See 1 Samuel 13:11–14; 15:10–11; 16:6–12.)

2. Even before David became a hero, what was his motivation? (See 1 Samuel 17:45–49.)

3. Saul hated David and tried to kill him various times (1 Samuel 18:10–11; 19:9–10). Read Psalm 62:4–8, which may have been written during this time. How would you describe David's state of mind while Saul was pursuing him?

The Judea Wilderness

4. For each of the following passages, describe David's circumstances and the "fortresses," or provision, that God made for him in the wilderness:

Scripture	Circumstance	God's Provision
2 Samuel 22:1–7		
Psalm 18:1–6		
Psalm 31:1–5, 9–13		
Psalm 71:1–4, 9		
Psalm 91:1–16		
Psalm 144:1–4		

Topic D: The Lord Is Our Rock

Many parts of Israel are quite rocky, especially the wilderness. This geographical condition, combined with the Hebrews' practice of describing spiritual reality by using the concrete images of the world in which they lived, led to the Jews' frequent use of the term "rock" to describe the character of their God. Let's look at some of these images.

1. When David was in the wilderness, to what did he attribute his safety? (See 2 Samuel 22:1–3.)

2. How do we know that David clearly connected the image of a rock with Israel's God? (See 2 Samuel 22:47; 23:3.)

3. Read each of the following passages and note what the image of God as a "rock" conveyed.

Psalm 18:31–35	
Psalm 62:1–2	
Psalm 62:5–8	

4. Which images did Moses use to describe God in Deuteronomy 32:4, 15, 18?

5. How did God describe Himself to the people of Israel through the words of the prophet Isaiah? (See Isaiah 44:8.)

6. Who does Paul describe as a rock in 1 Corinthians 10:1–4? What does he say that rock did?

Water from Rock

DID YOU KNOW?
David wrote these words: "I love you, O Lᴏʀᴅ, my strength. The Lᴏʀᴅ is my rock, my fortress and my deliverer" (Psalm 18:1–2). The word transliterated "fortress" here is really a rendering of a Hebrew word that can be translated *masada* in English. The psalmist recognized the solid, unmovable, unshakable characteristics of the Lord. He confidently placed his trust in the Lord, who is truly our fortress, too.

ʀaith Lesson

Time for Reflection

Read the following passage of Scripture and take the next few minutes to consider God as your *masada*, your fortress.

> I love you, O LORD, my strength. The LORD is my rock, my fortress and my deliverer; my God is my rock, in whom I take refuge. He is my shield and the horn of my salvation, my stronghold. I call to the LORD, who is worthy of praise, and I am saved from my enemies. . . .
>
> He reached down from on high and took hold of me; he drew me out of deep waters. He rescued me from my powerful enemy, from my foes, who were too strong for me. They confronted me in the day of my disaster, but the LORD was my support. He brought me out into a spacious place; he rescued me because he delighted in me. . . .
>
> To the faithful you show yourself faithful, to the blameless you show yourself blameless, to the pure you show yourself pure, but to the crooked you show yourself shrewd. You save the humble but bring low those whose eyes are haughty. You, O LORD, keep my lamp burning; my God turns my darkness into light. With your help I can advance against a troop; with my God I can scale a wall. As for God, his way is perfect; the word of the LORD is flawless. He is a shield for all who take refuge in him. For who is God besides the LORD? And who is the Rock except our God? It is God who arms me with strength and makes my way perfect. He makes my feet like the feet of a deer; he enables me to stand on the heights. He trains my hands for battle; my arms can bend a bow of bronze. You give me your shield of victory, and your right hand sustains me; you stoop down to make me great. You broaden the path beneath me, so that my ankles do not turn.

PSALM 18:1–3, 16–19, 25–36

1. David trusted God to be his "fortress." King Herod, on the other hand, trusted in Masada—the fortress-palace he built—and his own abilities. In what ways are you trusting God as David did? In what ways are you, like King Herod, trusting in the work of your own hands?

2. When Masada was captured, the Zealots who desired a political messiah died. How does their tragic ending relate to what often happens today when people place trust in their "masadas" instead of the living Messiah?

3. Think about a specific time when God was a "rock" in your life—or in the life of someone you know. What did you discover about God during that time?

4. In what practical ways do you depend on God to be your "rock" and fortress? Take a few minutes to describe what it means for God to be your "rock."

Action Points

Take a few minutes to review the key points you explored today, then write down an action step (or steps) that you will commit to this week as a result of what you have learned.

1. *God is our fortress. We are to trust in Him, not in our own efforts, for protection and strength.* In Psalm 18:1–3, David used the Hebrew word that is transliterated in English as *masada* to describe God as his rock and fortress—the strong, unshakable source of his protection and strength.

    In what way(s) do you live as though God is your fortress—your protection and security? In what way(s) do you tend to trust in your own efforts when facing difficult challenges?

2. *If we are to know God as our rock and fortress, we must open our eyes and hearts to the protection, strength, and freedom that Jesus offers.* Some Jewish people sought a military messiah who would deliver them from Roman oppression. Thus they misunderstood the gospel of the Messiah who came to sacrifice Himself on their behalf, and they lost their lives without finding real peace.

    In what ways do you find it easy or difficult to believe the Messiah as He truly is? In what ways do you try to conform Him to your own view of what you would like Him to be?

Are you willing to live according to the purposes and standards of God's kingdom, or would you rather pursue a different type of kingdom? Why?

3. *Our commitment to God needs to be more than just words.* The Zealots who fled to Masada believed it was wrong to owe allegiance to anyone or anything other than God, and they were willing to die for what they believed.

To what extent are you willing to owe and live out your allegiance to God alone?

How strong a commitment are you willing to make to religious freedom, for example, in order to safeguard it in a culture that may not recognize God and His eternal, spiritual truth?

DATA FILE

The Jewish Revolts

The Seeds of Revolt

After the Romans began their occupation of Judea in 64 B.C., the Jews became divided on how to respond:

Religious leaders, particularly the Pharisees	Most believed the Messiah would come from the Jewish people (God's instruments) and make Israel a great, free nation; condemned Rome's excesses; viewed Romans as oppressors punishing God's people for their unfaithfulness to the Torah
Sadducees and secular leaders	Many decided to cooperate with the Romans, who gave them various privileges (John 11:49–50)
Zealots	Proclaimed revolution to be God's solution to Roman oppression (Acts 5:37)
Essenes	Waited for the Messiah to lead a violent overthrow of the Romans and their Jewish supporters
Herodians	Were satisfied with Herod's dynasty (Matthew 22:16)

The Sparks of a Firestorm

- Jewish factions longed for various freedoms.
- Many so-called messiahs preached their own brands of salvation (Acts 21:38).
- During Feast days, especially Passover, nationalistic tensions escalated, so Rome increased its military presence.
- After Herod Agrippa I, grandson of Herod the Great, died in A.D. 44 (Acts 12:19–23), the Romans appointed a series of increasingly

(continued on page 58)

(continued from page 57)

cruel, corrupt governors to rule the Jews, adding to the confusion, hatred, and division.

- The paganism of Rome's culture offended the Jews.
- Assassins began killing Romans—and the Jews who cooperated with them. (Paul was arrested and accused of being a rebel. See Acts 21:27–38.)
- Jewish priests, who became more dependent on Roman security and support, became more corrupt. Jonathan the high priest was assassinated.
- Common people were attracted to the Zealots' radical approach.
- Felix (Acts 24) was replaced by Festus (Acts 25) as governor. Both were brutal but ineffective in quelling the rising revolt. Ananias, the high priest, used this opportunity to murder his opponents, including James (Jesus' brother) and many other Christians.
- Two priests who succeeded Ananias (each of whom was named Jesus) and their followers fought one another in the streets.
- Florus, a new governor, tried to stop the violence by flogging and crucifying hundreds of people.

The Revolt Begins

In A.D. 66, while Christians and Jews were being thrown to wild animals in Rome, a Gentile in Caesarea offered a "pagan" sacrifice next to the synagogue's entrance on the Sabbath. Jewish citizens protested, so Jerusalem authorities ended all foreign sacrifices in the temple—including those to Caesar.

Governor Florus, who lived in Caesarea, then raided the temple treasury in Jerusalem. When protesters gathered, Florus unleashed his troops on innocent civilians. More than 3,500 people were killed, including women and children. Hundreds of women were raped, whipped, and crucified.

In response, Jewish mobs drove the outnumbered Roman soldiers out of Jerusalem, stormed the Antonia (the Roman fort), and burned records of debts kept there. Zealots surprised the Roman garrison at Masada, occupied it, and then distributed its weapons to the Jews. One Zealot leader in Jerusalem was assassinated by another, who then ordered the slaughter of all Roman prisoners left in Jerusalem.

The Violence Escalates

When Gentiles in Caesarea learned about the violence against fellow Romans in Jerusalem, they killed about twenty thousand Jews within a day's time. Fifty thousand Jews were killed in Alexandria, and the slaughter of more Jewish people escalated throughout the empire.

Gallus, the governor of Syria, advanced on Jerusalem with the Twelfth Legion, but the Zealots destroyed his troops in the mountain pass of Beth Horon. For a brief time, the Jews kept their national freedom and all the captured weapons from the imperial legion.

Nero ordered his leading general, Vespasian, to end the Jewish problem. Vespasian began his campaign in A.D. 67 in Galilee, using his army of more than fifty thousand troops. Sepphoris, Jotapata, Gamla (where the Zealot movement began), and other towns fell. Many Jewish men were executed, often by crucifixion; Jewish women and children were sold into slavery or saved for the games in the arena.

Flushed with his success in Galilee, Vespasian then conquered the coast, including Joppa and the lands east of Judea. He captured Jericho (east of Jerusalem) and Emmaus (west of Jerusalem). After Nero's suicide in A.D. 68, Vespasian became the Roman emperor and left his son, Titus, to complete the campaign against Jerusalem.

Meanwhile, factions of Zealots, blaming each other for their defeats, fought each other in Jerusalem. Another self-proclaimed messiah fought the Zealots. Confusion and terror reigned. Apparently most Christians had already fled to the mountains, acting on Jesus' words (Matthew 24:15–16). The long separation of Jews and Christians had begun.

In A.D. 70, Titus arrived at Jerusalem with at least eighty thousand troops. He captured half the city, slaughtered its inhabitants, and built a siege wall around the remaining portion of the city. Trapped inside, Jewish factions continued to battle one another. People killed one another over scraps of food. Anyone suspected of contemplating surrender was killed. Dead people filled the streets, and Jews who did surrender were crucified just outside the walls. Josephus, the Jewish writer, reported that six hundred thousand bodies were thrown out of the city as a result of the famine.

(continued on page 60)

(continued from page 59)

The Revolt Is Crushed

Mid July: Roman troops recaptured the Antonia fortress.

August 6: Sacrifices ceased in the temple.

End of August (the ninth of Ab): Roman troops burned and destroyed the temple—on the same day of the year that the Babylonians destroyed it more than six hundred years earlier.

August 30: The lower city fell.

September: The upper city fell.

Titus ordered all buildings in Jerusalem to be leveled, except for three towers in Herod's palace. All the citizens of Jerusalem were executed, sold into slavery, or saved for games in the arena. Alleys were choked with corpses. Babies were thrown off walls. People were burned alive. Eleven thousand prisoners died of starvation while awaiting their execution. Josephus records that more than one million Jews died, and nearly one hundred thousand were sold into slavery.

A Final Stand

A few Zealots fled to Herod's fortress of Masada, hoping to outlast the Romans. In A.D. 72, the Roman Tenth Legion laid siege to Masada and, using Jewish slaves, built a wall six feet high and more than two miles long around the base of Masada's mountain plateau.

For seven months, the Romans built a siege ramp against the western side of the mountain and then used a battering ram to smash a hole in the fortress wall. The Zealots fortified the wall with timbers, which the Romans burned. So the Zealots in Masada committed mass suicide. Only two old women and five children survived to share the Zealots' story with the world.

A Tragic Postscript: The Second Jewish Revolt

Eventually the Romans built a temple to Jupiter on the Temple Mount, and Emperor Hadrian (A.D. 117–138) wanted to build a Roman city on Jerusalem's ruins. The few Jews who remained in Jerusalem declared Simon Bar Kochba, a descendant of David, as their messiah. He began a new resistance, and in A.D. 131 the Jews again revolted.

The Fortress Masada

Although Bar Kochba's revolt was initially successful, the Romans struck back swiftly with overwhelming force. Hadrian himself responded with the Roman commander Julius Severus. The Romans destroyed nearly a thousand villages, killing or enslaving any Jews who had not fled. By A.D. 135, the Second Jewish Revolt had come to an end. Jerusalem became Hadrian's Roman city, the Jewish religion was outlawed, and the Jews became a people without a land.

The revolt drove Christianity to the ends of the earth, and it became a largely Gentile faith. Only today are its Jewish roots being recognized. The descendants of the Pharisees established Rabbinic Judaism, the orthodox faith of Jewish people today. The Zealots, Sadducees, and Essenes are no more.

The Time Had Fully Come

Questions to Think About

1. When you are given a great deal of information that is completely new to you, such as when you are taking a class on an unfamiliar subject, what is the result? Do you usually understand it all right away?

2. What is required for you to learn new information and be able to use it in practical ways?

3. Describe how God has brought special people or experiences into your life at key times in order to teach you important lessons.

4. Have you ever wished that you and other Christians could retreat from life in the world and just focus on living a holy life? Is it possible for normal, ordinary people to live holy lives in the midst of a spiritually dark culture? Explain your viewpoint.

video notes

The Essenes

Their Community

Their Lifestyle and Practices

Their Beliefs

Their Great Contribution

Understanding God's Work in History

video Highlights

1. What new insights into the Dead Sea Scrolls and the Essene community at Qumran did you gain through this video?

2. Why is it significant that the Essenes developed theological concepts and practices that were similar to those of the early Christians?

3. The Essenes of Qumran resisted the Hellenism of their culture by separating themselves and moving to the desert in order to study. What are the benefits and the disadvantages of their approach?

4. Which beliefs and values of Christians today are similar to those of the Essenes? Did these similarities surprise you?

5. How do you feel as you realize how deeply the Christian faith is rooted in the Jewish people and culture even before the time of Jesus?

DATA FILE

The Dead Sea Scrolls: An Accidental Discovery

It was a typical day in the Judea Wilderness in 1947. Near an old ruin at the northern end of the Dead Sea that scholars would later recognize as Qumran, a Bedouin shepherd rounded up stray goats at the foot of barren cliffs. He noticed a small opening to a cave, and when he threw a stone into the opening he heard the distinctive sound of pottery breaking. After telling two other family members about his discovery, he returned home with his goats.

The next day, Mohammed edh Dhib squeezed into the cave, which was littered with broken pottery. Two of the ten intact jars contained a large scroll and two smaller ones, which the disappointed Mohammed showed to the other shepherds. Little did they know that they had just discovered incredible treasures—the book of Isaiah, the Manual of Discipline

(continued on page 66)

(continued from page 65)

(describing Qumran community rules), and a commentary on the book of Habakkuk!

Mohammed hung the scrolls from his tent pole in a bag for several months, then sold them to an antiquities dealer named Kando in Bethlehem. Kando found the cave, located additional scrolls, and then—after showing them to church officials at Jerusalem's Syrian Orthodox Monastery of St. Mark's—sold the three original scrolls to a Jerusalem antiquities dealer named Samuel for less than one hundred dollars.

As word of the discovery spread, Professor E. L. Sukenik of the Hebrew University purchased Kando's additional scrolls. Meanwhile, Samuel had taken the three scrolls to the United States and advertised them in the *Wall Street Journal* on June 1, 1954. Dr. Sukenik's son, Yigael Yadin, happened to see the ad and, through a middleman, purchased the original find for $250,000 and presented the scrolls to the State of Israel. Today, they are in the Israel Museum in Jerusalem.

The Bedouin from Mohammed edh Dhib's tribe soon located more caves near Qumran containing additional scrolls and thousands of scroll fragments. Soon an official archaeological investigation was launched, and the caves and nearby ruins were carefully examined.

The Caves of Qumran

Known today as the Dead Sea Scrolls, scrolls (mostly scroll fragments) were found in at least eleven caves near the ruins of Qumran. Among the six hundred scrolls represented, a few of which had been preserved in clay jars (the extremely dry climate aided in preservation), scholars have identified copies of all the books of the Old Testament except Esther; Jewish writings from other sources, such as the apocryphal book of Jubilees; and specific writings from the Qumran community that included Old Testament commentaries, liturgical writing such as hymns, and rules for community conduct.

The most well-known scrolls include the nearly intact Isaiah scroll; the Copper Scroll that describes sixty-four locations where temple treasures were hidden (none of which have been found); the Habakkuk commentary in which the prophecies of God's judgment are applied to the Romans and those who resisted the Essenes' beliefs; and the Manual of Discipline describing the rules of the Essene community.

The scrolls, among the most significant archaeological finds of modern times, have:

- Profoundly affected our understanding of biblical texts.
- Provided striking insight into the theological and cultural setting of Jesus' life, the early church, and the history of Judaism.
- Provided fresh insight into our understanding and application of the Bible's message.
- Affirmed the accuracy of the Scriptures. Until the Dead Sea discoveries, the oldest copies of the Hebrew Bible dated to approximately A.D. 1000. The scrolls take us back beyond 100 B.C. Scholars were amazed to find few differences between old and new texts—most involved spelling changes. Truly, "All Scripture is God-breathed and is useful for teaching, rebuking, correcting and training in righteousness" (2 Timothy 3:16). Although a follower of God trusts the truth of the Bible by faith, the scrolls confirm that our faith in the accuracy of the Bible is fully supported by scholarly evidence.

Author's Note: Scholarly debate continues as to whether the scrolls were written or used at Qumran, whether they were the product of the Essenes, and whether the Essenes actually lived at Qumran. The best evidence to

(continued on page 68)

(continued from page 67)

date indicates that the Dead Sea Scrolls were the product of the Essenes and were written or collected at the Qumran settlement. This writer considers this to be the best understanding to date. The actual contents of the scrolls, and the similarity of the writers' beliefs and practices to early Christianity, are subject to much less debate.

Biblical Books Recorded on the Scrolls	Number of Scrolls Found Per Book
The Psalms	36
Deuteronomy	29
Isaiah	21
Exodus	17
Genesis	15
Leviticus	13
Numbers	8

small Group Bible Discovery

Topic A: Lessons in the Wilderness

The "vast and dreadful" wilderness (Deuteronomy 8:15) had a profound effect on the people of the Bible. There, God disciplined them for their lack of faith, disobedience, and complaining so that they would learn to trust in His faithfulness. There they were transformed from a band of refugees into a powerful nation called to live in obedience to God in His chosen land.

1. Which of Israel's forefathers spent time in the desert in preparation for the missions God gave them? (See Genesis 12:1–9; 13:1; Exodus 3:1; 1 Samuel 23:14.)

Topography of Israel: New Testament

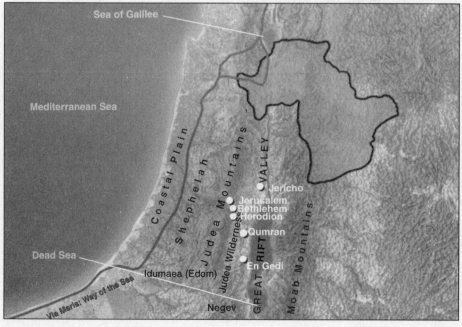

2. After God had delivered the Israelites from Egypt and provided their food and water for three months as they traversed the deserts, what did He do? Why do you think He chose that time and place? (See Exodus 19:1–6; 20:1–17.)

3. What do each of the following passages reveal about the Israelites' preparation in the wilderness?

   a. Deuteronomy 8:1–5, 10–18

   b. Psalm 78:9–18

   c. Psalm 95:6–11

   d. Jeremiah 2:1–2

DID YOU KNOW?

The landscape of Israel has played a significant role in biblical history and imagery. Much of Israel's terrain was rugged desert, referred to as "wilderness" in the Scriptures. These wilderness areas were located close to where most Israelites lived. The Negev Wilderness was barely forty miles south of Jerusalem, their holy city. The Judea Wilderness began just east of Jerusalem and was within sight of anyone who lived in the central mountains.

Because the wilderness, particularly the Judea Wilderness, was so close to settled areas, it became a refuge for those seeking solitude or safety from authorities. Here, David hid from Saul (1 Samuel 26), John the Baptist isolated himself from the religious practices of the day (Matthew 3), and Jesus faced the devil (Matthew 4). Here, the Essenes labored over their scrolls, and early Christians built monasteries, some of which still function today.

The Judea Wilderness

4. When the Israelites turned from God, what did the prophets call on the Israelites to do? (See Jeremiah 2:4–8; 31:31–32; Psalm 81:6–12; Hosea 2:14–15.)

5. What can Christians today learn from the experiences of the Israelites as they journeyed through the wilderness? (See 1 Corinthians 10:1–11.)

Topic B: The Way of Redemption Led Through the Wilderness

1. What role did the prophets say the wilderness would play in the coming of the Messiah?

   a. Hosea 2:14–23

   b. Isaiah 40:1–5

2. For what purpose did John the Baptist go into the wilderness? (See Matthew 3:1–3.)

3. Matthew 3:15–4:11 reveals that as soon as Jesus came up out
    of the Jordan River following His baptism, He was led into
    the desert—the same wilderness in which the Essene com-
    munity of Qumran was located—to be tempted by Satan.

    a. Why was the wilderness setting an appropriate place
        for Jesus' temptation? (See also Isaiah 40:1–3.)

    b. How did Jesus resist Satan's forty-day spiritual attack?
        (See also Luke 4:1–13.)

DATA FILE

Lessons of the Wilderness

The Hebrews' forty-year wilderness journey made such an impact on
them that later biblical writers and prophets referred to those days as
reminders of essential truths:

- The psalmist reminded them of God's faithful love that was demonstrated to them in the wilderness (Psalms 105:38–45; 107:4–9).
- Jeremiah (Jeremiah 2:6; 7:22–24) and Micah (Micah 6:3–5) reminded
  the people of the lessons they learned in the wilderness.
- New Testament writers compared the Israelites' wilderness experience
  to the lives of believers (Hebrews 3:12–19; 1 Corinthians 10:1–13).
- Jesus, the new "Adam," faced Satan on our behalf in the Judea Wilderness and used lessons from the wilderness to defeat him: "Man does
  not live on bread alone" (Matthew 4:4; see also Deuteronomy 8:3); and
  "Do not put the Lord your God to the test" (Matthew 4:7; see also
  Deuteronomy 6:16).

    c. Why did Jesus have to be tempted? What is the importance of Jesus' resistance to Satan compared with Adam's? (See Romans 5:16–19.)

    d. What do 1 Corinthians 10:13 and Hebrews 2:17–18 reveal about the importance of Jesus' temptation in the wilderness?

Topic C: A Community Set Apart to Fulfill God's Plan

God had worked for centuries to prepare the world for the advent of His Son, the Messiah. God had established His people Israel, the Promised Land, the line of David, the temple system, and even a small, wilderness community of devout Jews—the Essenes—to provide the cultural and theological context for Jesus' life and work.

The Essenes came into being in response to Hellenism, the secular worldview that swept the world around the first century. Hellenism glorified the human being, emphasized physical and sensual practices, and featured erotic themes celebrating the exploits of pagan gods and heroes. Many religious Jews abandoned their biblical worldview in favor of Hellenism. The Essenes, however, made a deliberate choice to remove themselves from Hellenistic culture and create communities in which they could worship and honor Yahweh. Their commitment exerted profound influence on the theological climate of their culture.

Thus, Jesus' message fell on fertile soil—prepared for more than a century by Essenes who waited expectantly for the Messiah to appear. The Essenes' beliefs, which were similar to many teachings and practices of Jesus and the early Christians, enhanced the popular acceptance of Jesus' message. Even today, the impact of their lifestyle and beliefs provides vivid insights into how God uses people through the events of history to unfold His plan of redemption. Let's take a closer look at how the lifestyle of this community helped to prepare the world to receive the Messiah.

1. The Essenes held all their personal possessions in common. In what ways was this similar to the lifestyle of the early Christians? (See Acts 2:42–45.)

2. The Essenes practiced a "ceremonial meal" that symbolized a great messianic banquet they believed would occur when the Messiah arrived. During this meal, they blessed bread and wine. What type of symbolic feast that Jesus established did the early Christians keep? (See Matthew 26:26–29.)

3. The Essenes practiced a ceremonial cleansing, using flowing water, that symbolized the spiritual cleansing brought about through repentance and forgiveness. What type of symbolic cleansing did the early Christians practice? (See John 3:22–23; Acts 2:37–41.)

4. The Essenes believed there was a great struggle between the sons of light (God's followers) and the sons of darkness (Satan's followers). What do John 3:16–21 and 12:35–36 reveal about the battle between good (light) and evil (darkness) in which the Essenes believed?

Qumran

1. Aqueduct and Reservoir System	3. Scriptorium	5. Potters' Workshop
2. Defense Tower	4. Main Assembly Hall and Refectory	6. Possible Mikveh
		7. Cemetery

5. What does Galatians 4:4–5 reveal about God's redemptive plan, including the part the Essenes played in preparing the Jews?

6. In light of Galatians 4:4–5, what does Romans 8:28 reveal about God's timing in the lives of His followers—including you?

Qumran: The Main Assembly Hall

7. God used the Essenes, who separated themselves from the world in order to know and worship God, to develop the practices and ideas that would help people receive the Messiah. In contrast, what did Jesus command His disciples to do so that they might continue to advance God's plan of redemption? (See Matthew 28:19–20.)

COMPELLING EVIDENCE

The Remains of Qumran

As is true with many ancient settlements, Qumran was destroyed and rebuilt various times. The earliest settlement on the site dates to the Israelite period shortly before the Babylonian Captivity (ca. 600 B.C.), when it was probably destroyed. Around 140 B.C., Qumran was resettled during the reign of the Hasmonaean king Hyrcanus, but the settlement was abandoned after a damaging earthquake (ca. 31 B.C.). Resettled about the time Jesus was born (ca. 6 B.C.), Qumran became an active community until the Roman army, under Vespasian's command, destroyed it in approximately A.D. 68.

The major structures in Qumran provide significant evidence of the lifestyle and beliefs of the community:

Aqueduct and Reservoir System

Water played an important role in the Essenes' theology. They believed that water used as a symbol of purification must be "living" or moving, not drawn by hand, so they developed a system in which rainwater ran on its own into a ritual bath. At least two cisterns were probably used as ceremonial or ritual baths (*mikvoth*) and had steps that allowed access to the water.

The Essene Water Tunnel

New members were cleansed with water in a type of baptism that apparently symbolized the spiritual cleansing that resulted from repentance and forgiveness after any breaking of God's laws. (See Matthew 3:6, 11.) The Essenes' ritual cleansing likely provided the background for the baptism practiced by John the Baptist and Christian baptism.

(continued on page 80)

(continued from page 79)

The Essenes' commitment to doing what they believed God wanted them to do is exemplary. They created catch basins just west of their community where runoff from the Judea Wilderness cascaded over a cliff. They tunneled more than one hundred feet through solid rock to bring the

An Essene Cistern

water to the cliff's edge, then directed the water through more than one thousand feet of plaster-coated channels and aqueducts until it reached the community, where it was stored in cisterns.

Defense Tower

Scholars debate the importance of the large tower that once stood in Qumran because it was essentially a religious community of separatists who lived a peaceful, almost monastic existence. The Essenes did, however, believe in the Messiah's imminent arrival and that a great battle would ensue between the sons of light (themselves) and the sons of darkness (followers of evil). The tower most likely provided protection against bandits or other less "military" threats.

Scriptorium

Archaeologists believe the Dead Sea Scrolls were written in this area. Excavation has revealed tables and benches similar to those used by scribes, as well as ink pots and basins in which the Essenes could ritualistically wash their hands before and after writing God's sacred name.

Main Assembly Hall and Refectory

In this room, archaeologists believe the Essenes practiced a ceremonial, communal meal in anticipation of the great banquet of the messianic age. Scholars have discovered many similarities between the

Essenes' ceremonial meal and the Last Supper recorded in the Gospels (Matthew 26:26–29).

In one corner of the room, a small water channel entered where the floor sloped down toward the opposite end of the room. This may have allowed the room to be washed in preparation for the meal. Nearby, archaeologists have unearthed a kitchen with five fireplaces and a smaller room containing the remains of more than one thousand pottery jars, dishes, plates, and cups. Interestingly, community members did not live in this or any other buildings uncovered by archaeologists. They probably lived in nearby caves or tents.

Potters' Workshop

Here, archaeologists have found a basin for preparing clay, a base for a potter's wheel, and two kilns. The clay jars, which helped to preserve the Dead Sea Scrolls for nearly two thousand years, were probably made here.

Cemetery

The main cemetery east of Qumran contains more than one thousand carefully arranged grave sites in orderly rows. Each grave was marked by a small mound of stones, and individuals were buried with their heads facing south. Although ancient writers, including Josephus, indicated that no women lived among the Essenes, several graves contained women's bodies. Scholars have suggested that these were family members of the Qumran community.

Topic D: The Essenes Prepare the Way for the Messiah

As they devoted themselves to God and the study of the Hebrew Scriptures, the Essenes developed theological concepts and terminology that are similar, or even identical, to those expressed by the New Testament writers. Let's consider the Essenes' understanding of theology and how it contributed to the people's ability to accept Jesus as the Messiah.

1. In the Dead Sea Scrolls, the Essenes used each of the following words or phrases, which are common to the New Testament but not elsewhere, long before Jesus was born. Match the words and phrases below to the following New Testament Scriptures: Matthew 3:3 (Isaiah 40:3); 5:3; 6:22–23; Luke 1:32, 35; John 1:5; 3:19–21; 12:35–36; 2 Corinthians 6:14, 15; Hebrews 7:1–3.

Words or Phrases Used by the Essenes	New Testament Reference
sons of light	
light and darkness	
Belial	
poor in spirit	
Melchizedek	
Son of God (Son of the Most High)	
way of the Lord	

2. How would the Essenes' use of the above words and phrases (and many others) have prepared Jesus' audience?

3. The Essenes interpreted prophetic Scriptures as being fulfilled by the events of their day, which differed significantly
   from other religious movements. Why was acceptance, or
   at least knowledge, of this concept important to God's plan
   of redemption? (See Matthew 3:1–3; Luke 4:14–21;
   18:31–33; Acts 2:14–36.)

WORTH OBSERVING

God's Perfect Timing

Scripture reveals that God arranged many significant events, movements,
and people in order to make the timing of Jesus' birth perfect for the
beginning of the church. According to Galatians 4:4–5, "When the time
had fully come, God sent his Son, born of a woman . . . to redeem." Timing-
related factors include:

- The conquests of Alexander the Great, 350 years before Jesus, which
  made the known world conversant in one language—Greek. This significantly increased the early spread of the Gospel (Acts 9:20–21).
- World dominion by the Roman Empire, which provided world peace
  and a wide network of roads, built for the Roman legions and trade,
  that the Christian missionaries would later use. The Romans also executed by crucifixion, and the psalmist had predicted that Jesus would
  be pierced at His execution (Psalm 22:16–17).

4. The Essenes traced the priesthood of the Messiah to Melchizedek, not Aaron. Why is this belief essential to accepting Jesus as the Messiah? (See Luke 1:31–33; Hebrews 7:1–22.)

5. Even though the Essenes had many beliefs in common with the early Christians, there were key differences between them. Compare the Essenes' belief in two Messiahs (a priest and a king) with Hebrews 7:15–17; 8:1–2; Luke 1:32–33.

WAS JOHN THE BAPTIST AN ESSENE?

Did John the Baptist live at Qumran? See the Dead Sea Scrolls? Write any of them? These questions have gripped scholars because the scrolls reveal remarkable similarities between the Essenes and John's teaching and practices. However, John was never identified as an Essene, was not a member of any community, can't be placed definitively at Qumran, and proclaimed his message publicly rather than seeking the shelter of a monastic setting. Note the following comparisons:

John the Baptist	The Essenes
Came from family of priests (Luke 1:5)	Many were priests who disagreed with temple authorities
Lived in the wilderness (Luke 1:80)	Qumran was in the Judea Wilderness
Was called to "prepare the way for the LORD" (Isaiah 40:1–5)	Lived in the wilderness to prepare the way for the Lord
Baptized as a sign of repentance and inner cleansing (Mark 1:4–5)	Practiced ritual cleansing in water as a sign of the soul's cleansing
Proclaimed that the One to come would baptize with the Holy Spirit (Mark 1:7–8)	Believed God would pour out His Spirit like water to cleanse perverse hearts
Was not accepted by most people (Matthew 21:32)	Complained that people ignored their teachings
Didn't participate in the normal lifestyle of his people (Mark 1:6)	Lived an ascetic existence; prepared their own food
His disciples fasted and recited prayers (Mark 2:18; Luke 11:1)	Fasted; had specific prayers
Was in conflict with Jerusalem authorities (Matthew 3:7–10)	Wanted to create a new temple and religious practices

faith Lesson

Time for Reflection

Read the following passages of Scripture and take the next few minutes to reflect on how God would have you bring His light into the world without compromising with an ungodly culture.

> This is the message we have heard from him and declare to you: God is light; in him there is no darkness at all. If we claim to have fellowship with him yet walk in the darkness, we lie and do not live by the truth. But if we walk in the light, as he is in the light, we have fellowship with one another, and the blood of Jesus, his Son, purifies us from all sin.
>
> 1 JOHN 1:5–7

> "You are the light of the world. A city on a hill cannot be hidden. Neither do people light a lamp and put it under a bowl. Instead they put it on its stand, and it gives light to everyone in the house. In the same way, let your light shine before men, that they may see your good deeds and praise your Father in heaven."
>
> MATTHEW 5:14–16

> The night is nearly over; the day is almost here. So let us put aside the deeds of darkness and put on the armor of light. Let us behave decently, as in the daytime, not in orgies and drunkenness, not in sexual immorality and debauchery, not in dissension and jealousy. Rather, clothe yourselves with the Lord Jesus Christ, and do not think about how to gratify the desires of the sinful nature.
>
> ROMANS 13:12–14

> Do not be yoked together with unbelievers. For what do righteousness and wickedness have in common? Or what fellowship can light have with darkness? What harmony is there between Christ and Belial? What does a believer have in common with an unbeliever? What agreement is there between the temple of God and idols? For we

are the temple of the living God. As God has said: "I will live with them and walk among them, and I will be their God, and they will be my people."

"Therefore come out from them and be
    separate,
                                    says the Lord.
Touch no unclean thing,
    and I will receive you."
"I will be a Father to you,
    and you will be my sons and daughters,
                        says the Lord Almighty."

Since we have these promises, dear friends, let us purify ourselves from everything that contaminates body and spirit, perfecting holiness out of reverence for God.

2 CORINTHIANS 6:14–7:1

1. Reread the first two passages above and meditate on what it means to you to have fellowship with God and to walk in His light rather than to walk in darkness. Consider also what being the light of the world means to you.

2. Which modern-day values or practices might be similar to the Hellenistic values the Essenes fled? What must you do to flee these values or practices personally, yet remain in the world as a light that shines forth and reveals God to a sinful world?

3. Select a portion of one of these passages that encourages you to "put aside the deeds of darkness" and live as a light

to the world. Place that passage in a place where you can read it frequently and take it to heart.

Action Points

Take a few minutes to review the key points you explored today, then write down an action step (or steps) that you will commit to this week as a result of what you have learned.

1. *God's work in history is rarely sudden and dramatic. Rather, God works through the process of history, through the lives of people, to unfold His plan of redemption.* Just as He used the Romans and the Essenes to prepare a culture and a setting in which the life, death, and resurrection of Jesus could be understood and received, He continues to use people to bring about His redemptive plans. So as we seek to understand the culture of first-century Israel where Jesus lived, we will gain a better understanding of His message.

   What does God's careful preparation for Jesus' coming reveal about His character? About the relationship He desires to have with you?

   Just as God used people, such as the Essenes, in biblical times to help bring about His plan for redemption, God wants to use you as well. In what ways might He be using you in His redemptive plan—among family members, at work, in your neighborhood?

2. *The Essenes, who recognized that spiritual light and spiritual darkness cannot coexist, committed themselves to godly values and beliefs and refused to compromise with their culture.* Today, we Christians face the same challenge: to seek to remove the spiritual darkness in our hearts, minds, and lives and to live as children of the light.

What personal compromise(s) do you make with ungodly values or beliefs? If you are willing, write out your commitment to remove that spiritual darkness from your life:

Dear Lord, I realize that if I am to shine as a light for You, I must put aside the darkness of _____. Help me to seek Your holiness, to "put on the armor of light" in every area of my life.

3. *Whereas the Essenes separated from their culture in order to study how to follow God, God has called Christians to carry His truths into the secular world.* Without compromising our holy calling, we are to interact with people who live in spiritual darkness and to confront evil in the world around us. We are to exhibit God's light to a watching, hurting world.

Which challenges do you face as you seek to obey and honor God and at the same time live among people who want little or nothing to do with Him?

Begin to pray specifically that God will encourage and strengthen you so that you can walk in His light and carry out His calling.

Instead of abandoning the secular culture, as the Essenes did, God calls you to take His light to people who live in spiritual darkness. Identify one individual with whom you could share God's light. Which step(s) will you take this week to bring God's light into that dark corner?

DATA FILE

A Brief History of the Essenes

In 332 B.C., Alexander the Great's armies swept through Israel, and his successors continued his campaign to bring Greek culture to every part of the known world. The Hellenistic culture deeply offended and disturbed devout Jews, but most of the Jewish people were soon seduced by this secular worldview that glorified the human being through philosophy, athletics, religion, and the arts.

Initially, Alexander's successors—the Ptolemy family from Egypt—allowed significant religious freedom for the Jews. During their rule, the Old Testament was translated into Greek, the translation we know as the *Septuagint*. Later, the Seleucids—Syria's Greek dynasty—brought Israel into their empire. They aggressively promoted Greek culture and defiled the temple in Jerusalem with pigs' blood and dedicated it to their god, Zeus. They banned the Torah, the Sabbath observance, and circumcision. To violate these bans meant death.

Faithful Jews, led by the Hasmonaean family (also known as the Maccabees) revolted. Through God's blessing, Judah Maccabee and his brothers drove out the pagans and reestablished Jewish independence for the first time in nearly five hundred years. The temple was cleansed and rededicated, and worship of Yahweh resumed. Their great victory became the focus of the Feast of Dedication, known today as Hanukkah (John 10:22).

The Hasmonaean descendants, however, became thoroughly Hellenistic. They openly flaunted pagan practices and fought bitterly with followers of the Torah. When Jonathan the Hasmonaean, who was a Hellenist and not from the line of Zadok (as required by pious Jews), assumed the office of high priest, that was the final straw. The Hasidim, a pious group of Jewish believers that had strongly supported the Maccabean revolt, openly opposed the descendants of Judah.

Out of the Hasidim came two movements that were very important to events of the New Testament: the Pharisees and the Essenes. Scholars believe that when Jonathan was appointed, the Essenes established a religious movement dedicated to the restoration of the true worship of God. Although Essene communities apparently were scattered throughout Galilee, Judea, and in Jerusalem itself, most Essenes (perhaps four thousand) lived in Qumran.

Believing themselves to be the sons of light preparing for a great battle with the sons of darkness, the Essenes felt they needed to be ready to take their place in God's army. Their mission was to prepare the way for the Lord. So they sought to keep their hearts and minds pure and their practices obedient. Stricter than the Pharisees in observing the Sabbath, the Essenes established many practices that set the stage for Jesus' arrival and teaching. They practiced ritual washing to purify themselves of sin, spent much time studying and carefully copying sacred texts, and practiced obedience to God and justice to humankind. Although they were small in number, they exerted significant influence on the religious community of their day.

In A.D. 68, the Romans destroyed Qumran. It is possible that the Essenes placed their sacred scrolls in jars and hid them in nearby caves as the Romans approached. Although this community has disappeared from history, its legacy is only now being realized.

No Greater Love

Questions to Think About

1. List some experiences that are common to many people in our culture today.

2. How would you use some of these common experiences to explain the gospel message to another person?

video notes

The Sermon on the Mount: God's Battle Plan

The Area of Jesus' Ministry: Korazin

Jewish Marriage Customs

Jesus Comes for His Bride

video Highlights

1. Look at the map of Galilee on page 95 of your Participant's Guide, and note the cities and towns of the region in which this video was filmed. Note the proximity of Capernaum and Korazin to the Via Maris, Bethsaida's location near Gamla and the Decapolis, and Tiberias across the Sea of Galilee from the Mount of Beatitudes.

2. What impressed you as you viewed the ruins of Korazin?

Korazin

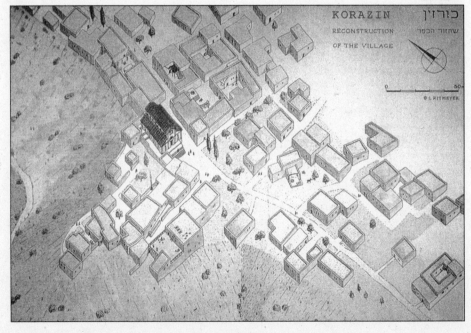

Galilee

3. What did you learn about the lifestyle and marriage customs of families in first-century Israel that enhanced your understanding of God's love for you?

4. Why should the Beatitudes be so important to Christians today?

DID YOU KNOW?

Jesus Probably Lived with His Extended Family

People in Galilee often lived in family housing complexes sometimes called *insulae* (singular: *insula*). Although not everyone lived this way, many people—particularly extended families—combined living units around an open courtyard. Jesus and His disciples may have lived in such a family compound in Capernaum. (See Matthew 12:46–13:1, 36; Mark 2:1–2; 7:17.) The insula provides the basis for one of the pictures of heaven (God's housing complex) mentioned in John 14:2.

In many places, the New Testament refers to "household," which means "an extended family living together." Jesus, for example, referred to various households (Matthew 10:24–25, 36). After Jesus healed the official's son, "he and all his household believed" (John 4:53). Peter described how an angel had appeared to a Gentile man and said that he (Peter) would bring a message through which the man and all his household would be saved (Acts 11:11–14). Paul and Silas told the jailer how he and all his household could be saved (Acts 16:29–32). (See also Romans 16:10; Ephesians 2:19; 1 Timothy 3:15.)

An Insula

small Group Bible Discovery

Topic A: Jesus' Relationship with His Bride—the Church

Jesus often used the metaphor of the marriage relationship to describe His love for His church.

1. In first-century Israel, a bridegroom's family agreed to pay a bride price (usually a large sum) to compensate the bride's family for the loss of their daughter. What price did Jesus pay for you? (See 1 Corinthians 6:19–20; Galatians 3:13–14; 1 Peter 1:18–19.)

2. An engagement in first-century Israel was as serious as marriage. (Breaking an engagement required a divorce.) After the families agreed on the "bride price," the couple drank a glass of wine together to indicate their life commitment to each other. How does your knowledge of this engagement custom enhance your understanding of Luke 22:20?

3. After his betrothal, the husband-to-be returned to his father's household and, supervised by his father, prepared a place for his bride by adding on to the family insula.

Where is Jesus, our Bridegroom, and what is He doing?
(See John 14:1–3.)

4. In first-century Israel, the bride-to-be remained at her par-
    ents' home, preparing for her wedding and learning how
    to be a wife and mother. One day, often in the evening, the
    husband-to-be and his friends and family would arrive at
    her home and announce their arrival with singing, danc-
    ing, shouting, and maybe even by blowing a trumpet. After
    the couple went to their new home and consummated their

Building a Typical Galilean Home

wedding, a lengthy celebration followed. How and when will Jesus, our spiritual Bridegroom, announce His arrival? (See Matthew 24:36–39; 1 Thessalonians 4:16–17.)

5. The parable of the ten virgins, recorded in Matthew 25:1–13, portrays the return of the bridegroom and the bride's need to be ready. In light of this parable, why must Christians always be ready for Jesus' return?

6. In light of the imminent return of Jesus, our spiritual Bridegroom, what should be our motive for godly living? (See 1 Corinthians 6:19–20.)

7. What does Jesus promise, according to Revelation 19:7–9; 21:2–4?

DATA FILE

Inside a First-Century Jewish House

In Galilee, the ancient village of Qatzrin has been excavated and recon-structed. Although it was populated centuries after Jesus' time, scholars believe that the buildings and artifacts discovered there represent the practices of the first century. Houses in Korazin, Bethsaida, and Caper-naum (where Jesus lived, healed, and taught) were also built in this style with these materials. By learning more about the homes and lives of everyday people in biblical times, we can better picture the living con-ditions with which Jesus was familiar.

A typical Galilean home was built of basalt (dark volcanic rock) and had either one or two stories. A stonemason (sometimes translated as a "car-penter") used a wooden scaffold as he carefully squared the larger rocks and wedged smaller stones in between to provide stability and strength. Sometimes walls were plastered with mud and straw. The doorframe was built of shaped stones and covered by a wooden door. A courtyard, located between various rooms of a family's housing complex, was paved with stones.

Roofs often were made of wooden beams topped with tree branches and covered with clay. When it rained, the clay absorbed water, sealing the roof. (In Korazin, however, roofs were made of stone slabs instead of branches.) Sometimes people did their work and slept on their roofs, which needed to be repaired every year. (See Matthew 24:17; Mark 13:15; Acts 10:9.)

A typical Galilean kitchen con-tained a domed oven for heat-ing and cooking when the weather was cold. Animal dung,

A Galilean Kitchen

the pulp of pressed olives, and small branches were used as fuel. Common kitchen utensils included hand grinders for making flour, cooking pots, reed or palm-leaf baskets for gathering and storing food, a broom, and stone water jars. Small gardens, vineyards with grapes and olive trees, and some small livestock provided most of the people's food. (See Luke 15:8.)

A Galilean family room, the center of family life, was probably used for eating, storing food, and socializing when the weather was inappropriate for being outdoors in the courtyard. Wealthy people reclined as they ate; poorer people sat on the floor or on benches. Food was served on pottery plates or in pottery bowls. Jewish laws regarding "clean" and "unclean" apparently required that different pottery be used for different types of food (so that meat and dairy did not mix, for example). (See Matthew 23:25; 26:23.)

A Galilean Family Room

Provisions such as grain, wine, and oil were stored in large jars in cool places. (See 1 Kings 17:7–14; 2 Kings 4:1–7.) Other foods were hung from the ceiling. Life for first-century Jews depended upon raising food and

(continued on page 102)

(continued from page 101)

Provisions

protecting it from spoilage, rodents, or insects, so the people needed to store it well. Jesus encouraged people to live by faith in God's provision, and He criticized people who were so obsessed with providing for the future that they hoarded goods. (See Matthew 6:25–26, 31–34; Luke 12:16–26.)

Sleeping quarters, sometimes located on the second floor and accessed by ladder, had beds made of wooden frames with rope stretched over them. A mat then was laid on each bed. Sometimes more than one family member slept in the same bed (Luke 11:5–7). Poorer people often slept on mats placed on the floor. People could take their mats with them when they traveled. (See Matthew 9:2–6; Mark 2:3–12.)

Lighting was often provided by small olive-oil lamps that were supplied from a goatskin oil container. Most people, however, went to bed at sunset and got up at dawn.

The Sleeping Loft

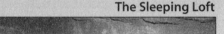

Honest people didn't work after dark, hence the phrase "works of darkness" was developed. (See Luke 22:53; Romans 13:12; Ephesians 5:11–14.)

A storeroom contained the all-important farming tools and supplies that most families needed in order .to provide

their own food: wooden plow, sickle, brooms, winnowing fork, a sieve for grain, rope made from plant fibers, an animal skin used as a churn for butter or cheese, etc. (The skin was hung and rocked for a long time in order to provide the churning action.) Typically a wooden plow with an iron point was pulled by a donkey or ox over the small fields in which grain was grown.

The Lamp

At harvesttime, farmers cut the grain with the sickle, then placed the grain on a hard stone surface called a "threshing floor" where it was crushed (threshed) by a small sled dragged by animals. Then the straw and grain mixture was thrown into the air on a windy day. The lighter straw and chaff blew away; the grain fell and was collected. Finally, the sieve separated any chaff that remained. (See Matthew 3:11–12; Mark 4:26–29.)

The Storeroom

Topic B: The Diverse Communities in Which Jesus Ministered

Many different types of people—religious and nonreligious, Jews and Gentiles, rich and poor, farmers and merchants—populated the area around the Sea of Galilee. Although certain groups tended to predominate in specific areas, people traveled from one area to another in order to hear Jesus and other rabbis teach. Despite His diverse audience, Jesus always tailored His messages appropriately to the beliefs and practices of people in the areas in which He ministered.

As you study this topic, locate each area on the map of Galilee found on page 95 of your Participant's Guide.

The Northwestern Shore of the Sea of Galilee

Home of Orthodox Jews, this area had many synagogues. The Pharisees, who were devoted to keeping God's Torah perfectly, predominated. People there knew the Scriptures and longed for the Messiah to come and relieve them of taxes and their scholars' endless debates.

1. Where was the "headquarters" for Jesus' ministry? (See Matthew 4:13–16.)

2. Where did Jesus perform most of His miracles, and what was the result? (See Matthew 11:20–24.)

Synagogue of Gamla

Northeastern Corner of the Sea of Galilee
Gamla, which was perched on a mountaintop in this region, was the home of Judah of Gamla, a Pharisee who started the Zealot movement. Although the term *zealot* technically applies to people who belonged to the movement that originated in Gamla, the term is often applied to all rebels who resisted Roman authority.

3. Where in this region did Jesus teach and heal? Why? (See Matthew 9:35–36.)

4. As Jesus demonstrated His miraculous power in this area populated by Zealots, what unusual request did He make? Why did He do this? (See Matthew 8:1–4; 9:27–30; John 6:14–15.)

Eastern Shore of the Sea of Galilee: The Decapolis

The Decapolis was an independent region of city-states established by Alexander the Great. For the most part, the people of this area were pagans who worshiped Greek and Roman gods.

5. Read Mark 5:1–20.

   a. Why did many Jews believe that demons lived in the Decapolis, where the "region of the Gerasenes" was located?

Susita in the Decapolis

b. What did Jesus tell the healed man to do? Why did His instructions differ from those He had given in the region of Gamla? What was the result?

Southwestern Shore of the Sea of Galilee

Herod Antipas, who executed John the Baptist, built Tiberias, his capital city, on the southwestern shore of the Sea of Galilee. Tradition holds that religious Jews would not live here during Jesus' time because the city was built over a cemetery. So the city's inhabitants were mostly secular Jews who supported Herod's dynasty, in part because of the economic and political power they enjoyed.

6. After Jesus challenged religious leaders to answer whether it was lawful to heal on the Sabbath, He healed a man's shriveled hand. How did the Pharisees respond? (See Mark 3:1–6.)

DATA FILE

The Way of the Sea

During biblical times, Israel was located at the crossroads of the world, where the trade of the civilized world passed through. Since the Arabian desert was in-between the empires of Egypt and Mesopotamia (Persia, Babylon, Assyria), the only trade route passed through Israel, a narrow land bridge between the Mediterranean Sea and the desert to the east. This busy road, the lifeline of the trade route, was known as the Via Maris, the "Way of the Sea."

Topic C: Jesus Presents His Battle Plan

For centuries, the people of Israel had longed for the coming of the Messiah and the establishment of God's kingdom. They had discussed these topics for generations. So when Jesus, the Galilean rabbi, taught that the kingdom of God had arrived, many people listened carefully. Although they longed for the kingdom of God, their idea of what it should be and how they should participate in it differed greatly from what Jesus taught.

So, as He taught in Galilee, Jesus clarified the true meaning of God's kingdom. In fact, we might view the Sermon on the Mount as Jesus' "blueprint" (or battle strategy) for kingdom living. He was willing to become God's sacrifice in order to usher in God's kingdom. What He commanded His followers, His *talmidim*, to do in order to participate in His kingdom was no less revolutionary. As we see more clearly how Jesus' presentation of kingdom living came across to the people of His world, we can better understand what it means to obey His call.

1. In Exodus 19:1–3 and 20:1–17, we read how God gave His law to Israel. Compare that event to the Sermon on the Mount, recorded in Matthew 5:1–12.

2. The twelve tribes of Israel received five building blocks: the Old Testament books of Genesis, Exodus, Leviticus, Numbers, and Deuteronomy. Without being too detailed, briefly describe Jesus' five great discourses, which are the building blocks for His followers.

Reference	Brief Description of Discourse
Matthew 5–7	
Matthew 10	
Matthew 13	
Matthew 18	
Matthew 24–25	

3. Consider how different segments of Jesus' audience would have responded to His unusual battle plan.

   a. What do you think the Zealots and the Pharisees may have thought when they heard Jesus speak of what is honored in His kingdom?

Reference	Zealots' Perspective	Pharisees' Perspective
Matthew 5:5		
Matthew 5:9		
Matthew 5:43–47		

   b. Read Matthew 6:19–24. How might the Sadducees and Herodians have responded to this message?

Topic D: The Burden of Those Who Refused Jesus' Message

Many people near the Sea of Galilee followed Jesus, witnessed His miracles, listened to His words, and became disciples. But others turned away from Him. To those, Jesus gave a strong warning.

1. Read Matthew 11:20–24.

    a. What caused Jesus to denounce the cities of Korazin, Bethsaida, and Capernaum?

    b. To which other cities did Jesus compare Korazin and Bethsaida? And Capernaum?

2. What were some of the sins of Tyre and Sidon? (See Amos 1:9–10; 1 Kings 11:33; 16:29–32.)

3. Which sins did the inhabitants of Sodom commit? (See Genesis 19:1–13 and Ezekiel 16:49–50.)

4. Do people commit the same kinds of sins today? What are some contemporary examples of these sins?

5. Why was the penalty Jesus pronounced for Korazin, Bethsaida, and Capernaum more severe than that for Tyre, Sidon, and Sodom—who were among the most evil peoples of the Old Testament? (See Matthew 11:21–23.)

6. In light of the above question, can we find people today who have heard all about Jesus but refuse to repent of their sins?

ғaith Lesson

Time for Reflection

Read the following Scripture passages and take the next few minutes to reflect on the ways in which Jesus has chosen to demonstrate His love for you, His bride.

> . . . You are not your own; you were bought at a price. . . .

> 1 CORINTHIANS 6:19–20

> "Do not let your hearts be troubled. Trust in God; trust also in me. In my Father's house are many rooms; if it were not so, I would have told you. I am going there to prepare a place for you. And if I go and prepare a place for you, I will come back and take you to be with me that you also may be where I am. You know the way to the place where I am going."

> JOHN 14:1–4

> "Be dressed ready for service and keep your lamps burning, like men waiting for their master to return from a wedding banquet, so that when he comes and knocks they can immediately open the door for him. It will be good for those servants whose master finds them watching when he comes. I tell you the truth, he will dress himself to serve, will have them recline at the table and will come and wait on them. It will be good for those servants whose master finds them ready, even if he comes in the second or third watch of the night. But understand this: If the owner of the house had known at what hour the thief was coming, he would not have let his house be broken into. You also must be ready, because the Son of Man will come at an hour when you do not expect him."

> LUKE 12:35–40

"No one knows about that day or hour, not even the angels in heaven, nor the Son, but only the Father. . . . Therefore keep watch, because you do not know on what day your Lord will come."

MATTHEW 24:36, 42

1. What does it mean to you that Jesus presents Himself as your spiritual "husband"—one who has bought you with a price and is even now eagerly preparing an eternal home for you?

2. What have you discovered during this session about the depth of Jesus' love for you? In what ways has His love for you as His "bride" been meaningful to you?

3. What is required for you to live every moment as one who is faithfully "engaged" to Jesus and who waits expectantly for Him—your Bridegroom—to return for you?

Action Points

Take a few moments to review the key points you explored today, then write down an action step (or steps) that you will commit to this week as a result of what you have learned.

1. *In order to communicate His deep love for us, Jesus described His love in terms of a family community—terms that His audience clearly understood. He compared Himself to a bridegroom who chose a bride (the church); who paid a steep price for her (His life on the cross); who has gone to prepare a place for her in His Father's house (heaven); and who will come again to take her home.*

   This metaphor was familiar to the people of Jesus' day because a bridegroom customarily left his fiancée to build a home for her, then returned to get her. Likewise, Jesus will one day return to take His followers to His home in heaven, where we will experience joyous community with Him forever.

   In what way(s) are you, if you are a beloved follower of Jesus the Messiah, preparing for His return?

   Which specific things will you do this week to better prepare yourself to be Jesus' bride?

2. *Through the Beatitudes, Jesus presented to His audience a picture of the lifestyle of the kingdom of heaven. In effect, the Sermon on the Mount outlined the "battle plan" for His kingdom. It gave His followers a new covenant—a new Torah, which, if followed, would change the world.*

    Which of the Beatitudes especially helps you understand how a person in Jesus' kingdom should live? Why is it meaningful to you?

    Select a verse from the Beatitudes to be your "motto verse" during the next several weeks. Read it several times a day.

    How will you seek to live differently in order to carry out that part of the battle plan?

The Rabbi

Questions to Think About

1. What risks does a deeply committed person take?

2. When a committed person crosses the line and becomes "fanatical" about something, what additional risks does he or she face?

3. What do you think attracts people to Jesus? What causes people to reject Jesus?

video notes

Gamla—Home of the Zealot Movement

The Synagogue—Center of Jewish Community and Religious Life

Jesus the Rabbi

video Highlights

Look at the map below and locate Gamla. Note its proximity to the Sea of Galilee and the towns of Bethsaida, Capernaum, and Korazin, where Jesus conducted much of His ministry.

1. What about Gamla surprised you?

2. Who were the Zealots, and what happened to them?

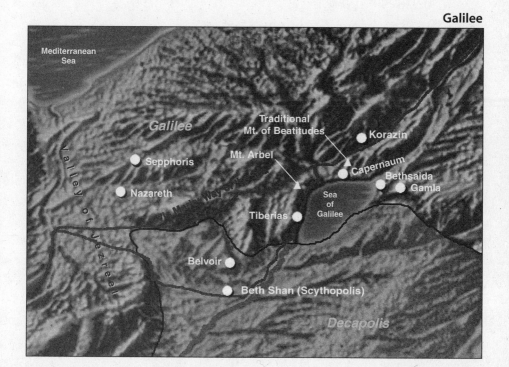

Galilee

Synagogue of Gamla

3. What new information did you learn about the Jewish synagogue?

4. In what ways was Jesus' role as a rabbi important to God's plan of redemption?

small group Bible Discovery

Topic A: The Lifestyle of a First-Century Rabbi

Jesus' role as a first-century Jewish rabbi provided the perfect setting in which to proclaim His message. Let's look at the lifestyle and teaching practices of typical rabbis who lived during Jesus' time.

1. What did many of the people who encountered Jesus consider Him to be? (See Luke 7:40; 12:13; 19:39.)

2. What do the following verses reveal about rabbis who lived during Jesus' day?

Scripture Source	The Rabbi's Life
Luke 8:1–3	
Matthew 26:55; Mark 6:6; Luke 4:14–16; 7:36, 40–47	
Matthew 13:1–3	
Matthew 11:29–30	
Matthew 10:1–4; 17:24; 20:29; Luke 5:27–28	
Luke 19:37; 23:49	

3. Each rabbi or teacher taught his disciples how the Torah should be obeyed. The system of obedience to the Torah was called the "yoke of Torah." Read Matthew 11:28–30 and answer the following questions:

   a. What was unique about Jesus' "yoke"—His way of obedience to God?

   b. Why was it meaningful for Jesus to describe His message in this way?

   c. How do you think Jesus' audience—common people, religious leaders, rabbis—reacted to this teaching?

THE TRUTH OF THE MATTER

To Be Called a "Rabbi"

In first-century Israel, the title *rabbi* meant "master" or "teacher." It was a term of respect or a description of activity. The position of "rabbi" didn't become an official office until after Jesus' time. Many diverse people believed Jesus to be a rabbi:

- A rich young ruler (Matthew 19:16–22).
- Pharisees who were experts in the law (Matthew 22:34–36).
- An unnamed man in the crowd (Luke 12:13).
- Sadducees (Luke 20:27–33).

Topic B: The Message of Jesus, the Rabbi

1. What was the basic theme of Jesus' message? (See Matthew 4:17.)

2. Capernaum, a small village in which Jesus conducted some of His ministry, was located on the northern shore of the Sea of Galilee by the Via Maris, the crossroads of ancient civilization (see map on page 119). Why do you think Jesus chose Capernaum to be the hub of His ministry— His "hometown"? (See Isaiah 9:1–2; Matthew 4:12–17.)

3. For what did Jesus strongly condemn teachers of the law and Pharisees? (See Matthew 23:1–7.)

4. In contrast to the way a true disciple of Jesus would respond to His teaching, how did the inhabitants of

Korazin and Bethsaida respond? (See Matthew 11:20–22.) In what way is this message important for people today?

5. Describe the astounding event that occurred one Sabbath in Nazareth when it was time for Jesus, the next scheduled reader, to read His assigned portion from the prophets. (See Luke 4:14–21.)

DATA FILE

What Is a Disciple?

The Hebrew word for *disciple* is *talmid* (plural: *talmidim*). This word stresses the relationship between rabbi (teacher or master) and disciple (student). A *talmid* of Jesus' day would give up his entire life in order to be with his teacher. The disciple didn't only seek to know what the teacher knew, as is usually the case in our educational practice today. It was not enough just to *know* what the rabbi said. Rather, the foremost goal of any *talmid* was to become *like* the rabbi and do what the rabbi did (Luke 6:40). The Pharisees, for example, knew and taught the truth (according to Matthew 23:1–4), but many of them were not Jesus' disciples because they did not obey God's teaching.

Jesus' disciples became like Him in various ways. For example, they performed miracles, loved their enemies, and were persecuted and killed for their faith. Today, Jesus calls us to be His disciples—to know His message, to share it with others, and to model our lives after His. (See Matthew 28:19–20; John 8:31; 13:34–35.)

6. Why did rabbis of Jesus' day wear the Jewish prayer shawl with tassels on it? (See Numbers 15:37–41.)

DID YOU KNOW?

Understanding a Great Miracle

During Jesus' time, Jewish men wore two garments: a light tunic and a heavy mantle worn over the tunic (*tallit* in Hebrew). Attached to the corners of the *tallit* were the tassels (*tsitsityot*) that God had commanded the Israelites to wear (Numbers 15:37–41; Deuteronomy 22:12). The tassels reminded people of their obligations to God to keep all of His commandments, were intended to direct other people to God when the Messiah came, and reminded people that God was with His people. (The hem also communicated the wearer's status or rank.) One of the threads on each tassel had to be blue, a reminder that the Israelites were royalty because they were a "kingdom of priests."

According to Jewish tradition, the Messiah would have "healing" in His "wings" as represented by the tassels (Malachi 4:2). This tradition helps us understand the story of the diseased woman who reached out to grasp the hem—the tassel—of Jesus' mantle (Matthew 9:20–22; Luke 8:40–48). Her action was a demonstration of genuine faith (Mark 5:34). By grasping the tassel of Jesus' garment, she was affirming the prophet Zechariah's message that God was with Him (Zechariah 8:23) and that He was truly the Messiah.

In this case, as in others recorded in Scripture, faith was essential to God's willingness to work His power (Matthew 9:29–30; Mark 10:52; Matthew 13:58). By grasping Jesus' hem, the ailing, "unclean" (Numbers 5:1–2), and nameless woman demonstrated faith in who Jesus was and what He could do for her. God in turn released His healing power and performed a miracle.

7. According to Jewish tradition, what was unique about the prayer shawl of the Messiah? (See Zechariah 8:23; Malachi 4:2; Mark 5:24–34.)

Topic C: The Zealots: No One But God

Jesus knew Zealots, addressed issues in which they were passionately interested, and shared their total commitment to serving God. Yet, His message about God's kingdom stood in stark contrast to their message, which advocated a violent overthrow of Roman oppression.

1. What did the devil tempt Jesus to do regarding God's kingdom? What was Jesus' commitment? (See Matthew 4:8–10.)

2. Consider how a Zealot might have received the following teachings of Jesus:

   a. Matthew 5:5

   b. Matthew 5:7

   c. Matthew 5:9

    d. Matthew 5:38–42

    e. Matthew 5:43–48

3. Why was paying taxes to Caesar an issue for the pro-Roman Herodians and the Jewish Zealots? How did Jesus answer the loaded question He was asked? How did it satisfy, or not satisfy, both groups? (See Matthew 22:15–22; Mark 12:13–17.)

4. As Jesus demonstrated His miraculous power, what unusual instructions did He give? What was He trying to avoid? (See Matthew 8:3–4; 9:29–30; Mark 1:40–44; Luke 8:51–56; John 6:14–15.)

DID YOU KNOW?

One of the men Jesus chose to be one of His disciples was Simon the Zealot (Mark 3:13–19). We do not know whether Simon gave up his support for Zealot tactics after joining Jesus, but the disciples' tendency to see the kingdom of God as a political entity may indicate Zealot influence. Some scholars believe that the reference to Simon as a "Zealot" meant that he was zealous. That perspective, although possible, is unlikely.

5. The word used to describe Barabbas in Luke 23:13–25 is the same word used to mean *Zealot*. What was the irony in Pilate's decision regarding Jesus?

DATA FILE

Who Were the Zealots?

In about 45 B.C., a Jewish patriot named Hezekiah led a band of freedom fighters against the Romans and their supporters. Herod the Great captured Hezekiah and executed him, as he did to thousands of like-minded Jews during his reign. Although devout Jews continued to bitterly oppose Roman rule and taxation, there was no widespread resistance movement until Judea was officially incorporated into the Roman Empire in A.D. 6. At that time, Judah of Gamla, the son of Hezekiah, urged violent resistance. Supported by a popular Pharisee named Zadok, also from Galilee, Judah led a revolt. Judah was killed, his followers were scattered, and the Zealot movement began.

The term *Zealot* technically applies to a person who belonged to the party or "philosophy" that began in Gamla, but it often is applied to all Jewish rebels who resisted Roman authority and Jewish collaborators. For generations, the Zealots violently resisted the emperor's authority. They longed for a messiah who would raise up a great army, destroy their Roman overlords, and reestablish Jewish rule in Israel.

The Zealots based their zeal for God on the action of Phinehas, Aaron's grandson, who used a spear to defend God's name and destroy unfaithfulness to Torah among the Jewish people (Numbers 25:7–13). The Zealots interpreted this action to be a divine command to use violent action to defend God's name, which led to a long history of violent acts against Rome and brutal conflict between the Zealots and the Jews whom they believed cooperated with the pagan empire.

The Zealots' creed can be summarized as follows:

- *There is only one God.* Exodus 20:3 revealed that "you shall have no other gods," so no one else could be acknowledged as king.
- *Israel is to serve God alone.*
- *The Torah and other writings of the Hebrew Bible are the only guide to righteous living.* The Zealots lived in strict conformity to the Torah.
- *Neither Rome nor Herod is a legitimate authority.* People are to use every means possible, including violence, to resist earthly authority.
- *Serving the Roman emperor in any way—whether in worship, slavery, or paying taxes—is apostasy against God.* Taxes are to be paid only to God.
- *Serving Rome, whether by choice or as a slave, violates God's supreme authority.*
- *God is on our side, so we will triumph in the end.* This belief led to the Zealots' reputation for incredible bravery and tolerance for suffering.
- *The Scriptures promise that the coming Anointed One will be a great military leader and king, like King David was.*

DATA FILE

The End of the Zealots

The Zealot minority, although certainly influential, did not have the means to defeat the Roman Empire. Having rejected the kingdom and peace that Jesus offered, they came to a tragic end:

- Judah of Gamla, the movement's founder, was executed. His sons, Jacob and Simeon, were both crucified in approximately A.D. 48.
- Menahem, another of Judah's grandsons whom some believed to be the Messiah, seized Masada in A.D. 66 during the first true military action of the Jewish Revolt. (The Roman weapons in Masada equipped the Zealots.) Another Zealot later murdered Menahem.
- John of Gischala, a Zealot, futilely defended Jerusalem and the Temple Mount until the Romans conquered the city.
- In A.D. 73, the Romans laid siege to Masada. Eleazar Ben Yair, a descendant of Judah of Gamla, held out until there was no more hope. Then the Zealots in Masada, the last remaining Zealots, committed mass suicide.

THE ZEALOT MOVEMENT

HASIDIM

Called the "Pious Ones," they resisted Hellenism by being totally devoted to Torah.
They fought with Judah and the Maccabees against the Syrian Greeks (Seleucids) in 167 B.C.

The Hasmonaeans, the Maccabees' descendants, became as Hellenistic as the Seleucid Greeks.

Hasidim became two movements.

PHARISEES

- Resist Hellenism and the pagan worldview
- Totally devoted to Torah

ZEALOTS

- Resist Hellenism and the pagan worldview
- Totally devoted to Torah
- Were terrorists

ZEALOTS

Hezekiah
- Resisted Rome and Herod (47 B.C.)
- Was executed by Herod

Judah of Gamla
- Attacked Sepphoris in 4 B.C. to gain control
  of its arsenal
- Founded Zealot party with Zadok the Pharisee in
  A.D. 6, at the time of the census
- Was probably killed by Herod Antipas (see Acts 5:37)
- Beliefs: 1. God alone may rule Israel
           2. Pay taxes to no one but God
           3. Slavery is worse than death

Sons of Judah

Jacob
- Crucified for terrorism
  in A.D. 48

Simeon
- Crucified for terrorism
  in A.D. 48

Yair

Grandsons of Judah

Eleazar Ben Yair
- Son of Yair
- Commander of Masada
- Committed suicide in A.D. 73

Menahem
- Leader of a revolt in Jerusalem
- Killed by opponents in A.D. 66

Topic D: Misunderstandings Concerning Jesus' Kingdom

1. What do the following verses reveal about how people mis-
    understood Jesus and His kingdom?

    a. *The disciples* (See Matthew 26:47–51; Mark 10:35–45.)

    b. *The Romans* (See John 18:33–37.)

    c. *The crowd in the Garden of Gethsemane* (See Matthew
        26:55–56.)

2. The Romans apparently feared that Jesus was a Zealot.
    Look up the following references to find evidence that
    could have raised their suspicions.

Scripture Reference	Was He a Zealot?
Mark 3:13–18	
Matthew 2:1–9	
Mark 11:15–18	
John 12:12–15	

3. To clarify what His kingdom was about, what did Jesus say to Pilate, who no doubt wondered if Jesus was the political-military king that the Zealots awaited? (See John 18:36.)

4. When Jesus appeared to His disciples after His resurrection, what did they ask Him that reflected the ideology of the Zealots? (See Acts 1:6.)

Topic E: Jesus Taught in Synagogues

The New Testament records more than ten occasions when Jesus ministered in synagogues, which provided a ready platform for His teaching. Imagine Jesus sitting on a stone bench or on the floor of a synagogue and listening, or on the *bema* (speaker's platform) holding the Torah scrolls. As we understand the role of the synagogues in Jewish life, we can better appreciate the actions and words of Jesus that took place there.

1. In which specific towns or regions did Jesus visit synagogues? (See Matthew 4:23; Mark 1:21; Luke 4:14–22, 44.) How important was the synagogue to His ministry?

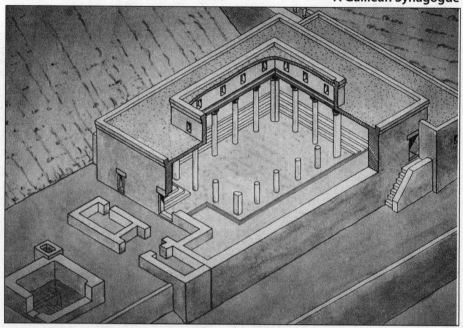

A Galilean Synagogue

2. Read the following Scripture passages and describe what
    Jesus' ministry in the synagogues involved.

Scripture	How Jesus Ministered
Matthew 12:9–13	
Luke 4:31–37	
Luke 4:16–22	
John 6:28–59	

DATA FILE

Synagogues of Jesus' Time

Synagogues have been a part of Jewish life since well before Jesus' time. They began as small assemblies of people for the purpose of study and prayer (perhaps as early as the time of Solomon's temple), and became particularly important during the Babylonian exile following the destruction of the first temple in Jerusalem. In Babylon, the Jews met regularly to study the Torah and reflect on the need to be obedient to God. The synagogue developed out of these regular meetings, becoming the center of Jewish social life as well as a place of study and prayer. The synagogue provided a place for the Jewish people to assemble and maintain their identity in a pagan land.

Even in the first century, the synagogue remained the focal point of Jewish community life. The synagogue served as school, meeting place, courtroom, seat of government, place of prayer, center for community celebrations, and in some cases may have provided lodging for travelers. In typical Galilean towns, synagogues occupied prominent places on an elevated platform in the town center or on the highest point in town, symbolizing the importance of living in the presence of God.

Outside each synagogue was a *mikveh* (plural: *mikvoth*) or ritual bath where worshipers symbolically cleansed their hearts before entering the synagogue. The *mikveh* had to be hewn out of rock or placed into the ground, and the water had to be "living"—flowing freely into the *mikveh* without being drawn. This tradition was in keeping with laws of the Torah regarding contact with "unclean" things (Numbers 19), bodily fluid (Leviticus 15), or other defiling objects such as idols.

The synagogue, a kind of democracy, was governed by local elders. Males thirteen years old or older could belong to it. A local ruler, called the *hazzan*, maintained the building and organized the prayer services (Mark 5:22, 35–38; Luke 13:14). He often taught in the synagogue school (especially in smaller villages), announced the arrival of the Sabbath with blasts on the shofar (ram's horn) on Friday evenings, and cared for the Torah scrolls and other sacred writings and brought them out at appropriate times (Luke 4:16–21).

Inside the synagogue, the leader of the service sat on a small, elevated platform on which a reading table, a menorah (a seven-branched candlestick), and a seat (sometimes referred to as the Moses' seat—Matthew 23:2) may have been placed. The members of the synagogue either sat on the floor or on stone benches or steps against the walls (the chief seats were those on the stone benches—Matthew 23:6). Common people sat on mats on the floor, which was usually paved with flagstones (although it was sometimes dirt and in later synagogues could have been an elaborate mosaic floor). Torah scrolls were kept in a permanent (but portable) chest called the holy ark—after the original ark of the covenant in which Moses placed the tablets of the law.

3. After the Babylonians destroyed the Temple in Jerusalem, the Jews could no longer worship God as they had for centuries. So they focused on studying God's law and making a different kind of sacrifice. What was that "new" sacrifice? (See Psalm 51:16–17; Isaiah 1:11–17.)

4. What did the apostle Paul express concerning the way in which Christians sacrifice to God? (See Romans 12:1–2, 9–21.)

DID YOU KNOW?

A Synagogue Education

Only boys attended synagogue schools. According to the Mishnah (the written record of the oral traditions of Jesus' time and afterward), students followed a specific educational plan. Since the learning of the community was passed orally, memorization of tradition and God's Word were essential. A typical education for a boy went as follows:

- At age five or six began memorizing and studying the written Torah.
- At age twelve studied the more complicated oral interpretations of the Torah.
- Became a religious adult at age thirteen.
- At age fifteen, a gifted student might continue his studies with a local rabbi in *beth midrash* (meaning "house of study" or secondary school), where he learned to apply the Torah and oral tradition to specific situations.
- The most gifted students would travel with famous itinerant rabbis, learning to understand and apply Torah and oral tradition in daily situations and seeking to "become like their rabbis."
- Learned a trade at age twenty.
- Demonstrated his full ability at age thirty.

By the time a student reached adulthood, he knew most Scriptures by heart and could tell whether someone quoted them correctly. Thus Jesus, in keeping with His culture, could say, "It is written . . ." and know that His audience would recognize an accurate quotation.

HIGHLIGHTS OF SABBATH WORSHIP

- Took place on Saturday morning in the synagogue.
- Began with several blessings offered to God, followed by the Shema: "Hear, O Israel: The LORD our God, the LORD is one" (Deuteronomy 6:4).
- The person selected to read the Torah would sit on the stone "Moses' seat" until the *hazzan* (temple ruler) brought the Torah scrolls. Then, the reader would stand up to read the words of Moses (Luke 4:16–21).
- As many as seven portions of Torah were read by different members of the synagogue community.
- A selection from the prophets was then read.
- A short sermon was offered. Interestingly, any member of the synagogue community could deliver the sermon. Often someone recognized for his wisdom and insight, or a visitor, offered the sermon. Even boys over age thirteen could, with permission, read or speak during the service. In this way, the community encouraged its youngest members to actively participate in its religious life.
- The service ended with a benediction. If a priest was present, he would offer the blessing of Aaron from the Torah (Numbers 6:24–26) at the end of the service. Aside from offering this blessing, priests and Levites could participate, but had no special role in synagogue life.

faith Lesson

Time for Reflection

Read the following passages of Scripture and take the next few minutes to consider what it means to be a disciple of Jesus.

To the Jews who had believed him, Jesus said, "If you hold to my teaching, you are really my disciples. Then you will know the truth, and the truth will set you free."

They answered him, "We are Abraham's descendants and have never been slaves of anyone. How can you say that we shall be set free?"

Jesus replied, "I tell you the truth, everyone who sins is a slave to sin. . . . So if the Son sets you free, you will be free indeed."

JOHN 8:31–34, 36

"Come to me, all you who are weary and burdened, and I will give you rest. Take my yoke upon you and learn from me, for I am gentle and humble in heart, and you will find rest for your souls. For my yoke is easy and my burden is light."

MATTHEW 11:28–30

When he had finished washing their feet, he put on his clothes and returned to his place. "Do you understand what I have done for you?" he asked them. "You call me 'Teacher' and 'Lord,' and rightly so, for that is what I am. Now that I, your Lord and Teacher, have washed your feet, you also should wash one another's feet. I have set you an example that you should do as I have done for you. . . .

A new command I give you: Love one another. As I have loved you, so you must love one another. By this all men will know that you are my disciples, if you love one another."

JOHN 13:12–15, 34–35

1. What is the true freedom that Jesus offers to His disciples? How is this like or unlike the freedom desired by the people of Jesus' day?

2. How is the freedom Jesus offers like or unlike the freedom you desire? Do you accept His offer, or are you holding out for a different kind of freedom?

3. In your own words, summarize the "yoke" that a *talmid*, a disciple of Jesus, takes on.

WORTH OBSERVING

The Roots of Christian Community

The earliest Christians attended synagogues, although they had a new interpretation of the Torah since Jesus had been revealed as Messiah (Acts 13:14). It appears that the early church patterned itself after the synagogue, continuing the same practice of living and worshiping together as a community (Acts 2:42–47). Jesus' followers today, who have been made one body because of Jesus (1 Corinthians 12:12–13), would do well to remember that the roots of the church are in community living and worship. In our fractured, broken world, the picture of the community of God—the model of the synagogue—is one we would do well to put into practice.

4. As people look at you and your lifestyle, is it obvious that you are a disciple of Jesus? Why or why not?

5. What changes in thought, word, and action do you need to make so that other people will know you are a *talmid* of Jesus?

Action Points

Take a few minutes to review the key points you explored today, then write down an action step (or steps) that you will commit to do this week as a result of what you have learned.

1. *Jesus came to earth to minister amidst a cauldron of conflicting ideas and tumultuous politics. Surrounded by a diverse array of belief systems, He assumed the role of a Jewish rabbi and taught a simple message that directed people toward fellowship with God. He also modeled the lifestyle of the kingdom of God and linked people's acceptance of His claim to be the Messiah to their willingness to follow the lifestyle He demonstrated.*

    Consider your lifestyle. In what ways does your life—at home, among friends, in the workplace—clearly direct people toward God?

Choose one aspect of your lifestyle that falls short of revealing the kingdom of God. What will you commit to do this week to more closely follow the lifestyle Jesus demonstrated?

2. *The way Jesus chose to point people toward God was to love them—even those whose inner hurt and brokenness led them to do things that were considered to be unacceptable or immoral.*

As His followers, we, too, are to point people toward God. Although using the tools of our culture to teach people about God is certainly important, our ultimate focus has to be on the hurts, needs, and cares of people and to minister to them as Jesus did.

Have you ever fallen into the trap of teaching about the kingdom of God while neglecting to truly love the people to whom you are ministering? What must you do to avoid treating people like that in the future?

What are the hurts, needs, and cares of some of the people God has brought across your path? In what ways, using the example of Jesus' life, can you reach out to touch the hearts of these hurting, needy people?

Language of culture

Questions to Think About

1. Have you experienced a situation in which you tried to communicate with another person, but you kept "missing" each other and couldn't seem to understand the other person's perspective? Describe what that was like.

2. Identify some groups of people within our culture that have diverse life experiences or differing beliefs and therefore don't "speak the same language" or have difficulty understanding one another.

3. Think about Jesus' life and list some of the different kinds of people to whom He ministered. What do you think enabled Him to communicate effectively to those people?

video notes

Sepphoris, a City of the Herod Dynasty

Jesus

A Tekton of Nazareth

Understanding His Culture

Impacting His World

video Highlights

Look at the map of Herod the Great's kingdom below. Note the specific territories for which each of Herod's four immediate successors was responsible.

1. In what ways do you think growing up so close to Sepphoris benefited Jesus and His ministry?

2. What did you learn about Jesus' vocation?

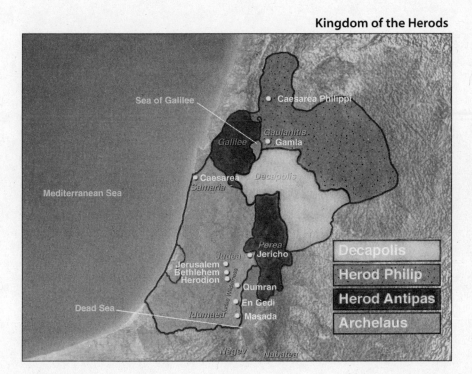

Kingdom of the Herods

3. What did the examples of Jesus' teaching that Ray Vander Laan cited tell you about Jesus?

4. Why is understanding culture well, according to this video, so important in ministering to people and reaching them effectively with the message of Christ?

small Group Bible Discovery

Topic A: The Significance of Nazareth

1. The small village of Nazareth in Lower Galilee was where Joseph and Mary made their home. At the time of Jesus' birth, they were in Bethlehem for the census required by Caesar Augustus. They had been told by angels that Jesus was the Son of God who would save His people from their sins. When King Herod sought to kill the infant Jesus, an angel warned Joseph and the family fled to Egypt, where they remained until Herod died and an angel told Joseph to return to Israel. (See Matthew 1:18–2:20; Luke 1:26–38.)

   a. When Joseph brought Mary and Jesus back to Israel, where did they settle? (See Matthew 2:21–23.)

b. Why was it important for them to live in Nazareth?
   (See Matthew 2:23.)

2. Since there is no record of a prophet specifically saying,
   "He will be called a Nazarene," let's explore the way in
   which Jesus' identity as a Nazarene fulfilled prophecy.

   a. How was Jesus identified by the people of His day? (See
      Mark 14:67; 16:6; Luke 4:34.)

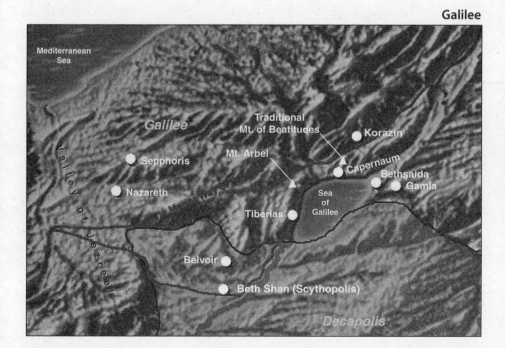

Galilee

b. The meaning of the word *Nazareth* is necessary to our understanding of how Jesus fulfilled the words of the prophets. The Greek word translated *Nazareth* (or *Nazarene*) is most likely derived from the Hebrew word *netzer*, which means "shoot" or "branch" and is frequently used to refer to the royal line of David. In the following Scripture references, note the expressions the prophets used to describe the Messiah:

Prophecy	Expression Related to the Messiah
Isaiah 11:1–2	
Isaiah 53:2	
Jeremiah 23:5	
Jeremiah 33:15	
Zechariah 3:8	
Zechariah 6:12	

c. The description "Jesus the Nazarene," meaning "Jesus the Branch," clearly linked Jesus to the prophecies stating that the Messiah would be the "Branch" that would grow out of Jesse's stump. What did Jesus say about Himself to confirm this identity? (See Revelation 22:16.)

DATA FILE

Sepphoris—A Window into Jesus' World

Sepphoris, like many cities of its day, had a tumultuous history:

- When Rome first invaded Israel, the Roman commander Pompey designated Sepphoris as the district capital of Galilee.
- Dating from at least the Hasmonaean period, the city was perched on top of a high hill surrounded by fertile, farm-dotted valleys.
- The inhabitants of the city resisted Herod the Great, however, so he slaughtered them in 37 B.C. and destroyed their city.
- People rebuilt Sepphoris and, led by the Zealots, its inhabitants revolted against Rome following Herod the Great's death in 4 B.C.
- Roman troops conquered and destroyed the city again.
- When Herod Antipas became king of Galilee, he began rebuilding Sepphoris as his capital.

Crowned by Herod's elaborate palace, Sepphoris was home to one of the largest theaters of the first century. The city was laid out in the latest Roman pattern with a colonnaded street leading to the forum. It also featured a gymnasium, an elaborate water system, and probably a bathing complex. Just three miles away, in the humble village of Nazareth, lived a Jewish boy—a stonemason by trade—who became known as Jesus of Nazareth. The beautiful and exciting city of Sepphoris, with its Hellenistic ideas, wealth, and power certainly impacted Nazareth and exposed Jesus to secular culture at a relatively young age.

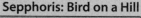

Sepphoris: Bird on a Hill

3. Based on their name and their Davidic lineage, the Nazarenes believed that the Messiah would come from their village because they were the "shoot" village.

    a. What does Luke 4:16–21 tell us about the Nazarenes?

    b. What did other people think of Nazareth? (See John 1:46.)

Topic B: Understanding Our Relationship to Jesus, the Image of the Olive Tree

When olive trees grow old, their branches no longer produce fruit, so the farmer will cut off those branches, leaving a stump several feet

The Olive Tree

wide and tall. Soon, new shoots begin to grow out of the old stump, and new branches are sometimes grafted onto the old stump. The prophets, Jesus, and the apostle Paul used this image, which was familiar to the people of Jesus' day, to help explain His relationship to His people.

1. In order to understand the metaphor of the olive tree, we must know what it represents. What is the identity of the "stump" and the "shoot"? (See Isaiah 11:1–3.)

2. In John 15:1, Jesus identifies Himself with the tree.

   a. What does Jesus reveal about God's relationship to the tree?

   b. What must God, the gardener, do to the "tree" that will not produce good fruit? (See Matthew 3:10; 7:19.)

   c. Has God ever had to do this? What was the result? (See Isaiah 6:11–13.)

3. What were early Christians called, and what did that description mean? (See Acts 24:5; Jeremiah 33:15.)

4. Romans 11:13–24 describes the relationship between Jesus the Nazarene, the Jewish people, and Gentile Christians. Fill in the blanks in the following:

    a. Gentile Christians are not "natural" branches of the stump. They are _____ that have been _____ among the others. (See Romans 11:17.)

    b. Gentile Christians share in the _____ from the olive root and must remember that they do not _____ the root, but in fact receive _____ the root. (See Romans 11:17–18.)

5. Gentile Christians, like Israel, are expected to produce fruit.

    a. What enables the branches to produce fruit? (See John 15:4–5.)

    b. What will happen to branches that do not produce fruit? (See John 15:6; Romans 11:21–22.)

Topic C: Jesus the Master Builder

Although Jesus was a trained *tekton* who could build with any material, He probably spent much of His time working as a stonemason, shaping and laying stones. Let's look at some of the images from the construction world that Jesus used as He taught His varied audiences.

1. On what did Jesus say He would build His church? (See Matthew 16:18.)

2. After seeing the spectacular construction of Herod's temple, what claim did Jesus make? What impact did it have on His audience? (See John 2:19–22.)

3. When addressing His disciples about their commitment to follow Him, Jesus drew an analogy between building a tower and becoming His disciple. What was His point? (See Luke 14:28–30.)

4. Read Matthew 21:42; Acts 4:11–12.

   a. With which part of a building did Jesus identify Himself?

   b. What does this metaphor say about His role?

5. Following Jesus' example, Peter also used images from stone construction to explain what it means to participate in the kingdom of God. (See 1 Peter 2:4–8.)

   a. Who (or what) is Jesus in Peter's analogy?

    b. What is Jesus the *tekton* building today, and with whom?

    c. What is Jesus to those who reject Him?

Topic D: Jesus and the Herods

From His birth until His death, Jesus' life on earth was intertwined with that of the Herod dynasty—Herod the Great, Herod Archelaus, Herod Antipas. Let's consider how Jesus may have been familiar enough with them to refer to them in His teaching.

1. What was the response of Herod the Great to the birth of Jesus, the "king of the Jews"? (See Matthew 2:1–8, 12–18.)

2. When Joseph moved his family back to Israel, what caused him to settle in Nazareth, thereby fulfilling prophecy? (See Matthew 2:19–23.)

3. The lives of Herod Antipas and Jesus were closely intertwined. Herod Antipas was the only Herod to meet Jesus
   face-to-face. Let's take a closer look at their relationship.

   a. After Herod Antipas had John the Baptist killed, what
      impact did Jesus' ministry have on him? (See Matthew
      14:1–2; Mark 6:14–16.)

   b. What was Herod Antipas's attitude toward Jesus after
      John's death? (See Luke 9:7–9; 13:31.)

   c. When Pilate sent Jesus to Herod Antipas, how did they
      respond to each other? (See Luke 23:8–11.)

4. What great irony concerning the relationship between
   Herod Antipas and Jesus is revealed in Luke 8:1–3?

THE HEROD FAMILY TREE

Antipater (Idumaean)

HEROD THE GREAT

- Died in 4 B.C.
- Effective administrator, cruel, supported by Rome
- Visited by wise men, killed Bethlehem babies
- Greatest builder the ancient Near East ever knew
- Had 10 wives, three of whom were:

Cleopatra	Miriam	Malthace
PHILIP	**ANTIPAS**	**ARCHELAUS**

PHILIP
- Effective, popular king
- Ruled north and east of Galilee
- Built Caesarea Philippi

(Luke 3:1)

ANTIPAS
- Effective king
- Ruled Galilee and Perea
- Killed John the Baptist
- Built Tiberias and Sepphoris
- Tried Jesus before crucifixion

(Luke 3:19; Luke 23:7–12; Luke 9:7–9; Matthew 14:1–12; Luke 13:32)

ARCHELAUS
- Poor ruler, deposed by Romans
- Ruled Judea
- Mary and Joseph settle in Nazareth to avoid him

(Matthew 2:22)

HEROD AGRIPPA I

(Grandson of Herod the Great)

- King of Judea
- Killed James, put Peter in prison
- Struck down by an angel

(Acts 12:1–24)

AGRIPPA II	**DRUSILLA**	**BERNICE**
	└──── *(Sisters of Agrippa II)* ────┘	

AGRIPPA II
- King of Judea
- Paul defends his faith before him

(Acts 25:13–26:32)

DRUSILLA
- Married Felix, the Roman governor

(Acts 24:24)

BERNICE
- With her brother at Paul's defense

(Acts 25:13)

DID YOU KNOW?

In Jewish culture, the fox was sometimes compared to a lion. The fox was small and weak, although he might act like a powerful lion. Whereas great people are like lions in that they make good on their talk, petty nobodies who put on airs and pretend to be greater than they are resemble foxes. A fox is someone who acts big and talks big but is really a "nobody." A lion can make good on his talk because he is truly strong.[1] Jesus may also have been referring to the fact that Herod was only a tetrarch, not a king.

[1]From an article entitled: " That Small Fry Herod Antipas, or When a Fox Is Not a Fox" by Randall Buth.

5. When Pharisees warned Jesus that Herod wanted to kill Him, what did Jesus say about Herod and about being in control of doing what God had called Him to do? (See Luke 13:31–33.)

6. How did the Herodians, the aristocratic Jews who supported Herod, respond to Jesus? Why? (See Matthew 22:15–22; Mark 3:6; John 11:49–50.)

PROFILE OF A DYNASTY

The Legacy of Herod the Great

Few families in history have come as close to Jesus' message as the Herods. Many members of this ruling family knew of Jesus and His followers. Yet, one after the other, they killed or tried to kill anyone connected to Him. Maybe the Herod family, descended from Esau and Edom, simply fulfilled the prophecies (Genesis 25:23; Numbers 24:17; Obadiah 8–21).

Ruler	Notable Deeds	Last Days
Antipas: ruled Galilee and Perea 40+ years	Brought peace and prosperity; sensitive to Jewish religion yet married brother Philip's wife; built Sepphoris and Tiberias; had John the Baptist beheaded; met Jesus and plotted His death (Jesus opposed him)	Agrippa accused him of a plot; new emperor exiled him and claimed his property
Archelaus: ruled Judea, Samaria, Idumaea 10 years	Killed families of Jewish delegations who had gone to Rome to accuse him; known for his bloodthirstiness and evil qualities	Exiled to Gaul, then disappeared from history
Philip: ruled area north and east of the Sea of Galilee 37 years	A just ruler who mainly governed Gentiles; peace-loving	Died of natural causes at end of his reign
Agrippa I: ruled area north and east of Sea of Galilee, Judea 8 years	Ruled a large area; sought to stop Jesus' followers; killed James and imprisoned Peter and other disciples	An angel of God struck him down; eaten up by worms and died
Agrippa II: ruled small portion of his father's region, had limited rule in Jerusalem	Advanced Hellenistic culture; wounded during Jewish Revolt supporting Rome; heard Paul's stirring presentation of the gospel in Caesarea, but was not persuaded	Was wounded fighting for Rome against the Zealots at Gamla, but the specifics of his death are not known

Topic E: Cultural Images in Jesus' Teaching

Jesus used word pictures and ideas designed to communicate effectively to His audiences. Let's now consider several elements of the world of wealth and power that were part of Jesus' teaching.

Royalty

1. Read Luke 19:11–27 and compare the parallels between Jesus' parable about the man of noble birth and widely known facts concerning Herod Archelaus:

Details in Jesus' Parable	True Herodian Facts
Luke 19:12:	Archelaus, a son of Herod the Great, went to Rome to request more land to govern than his father had bequeathed in his will.
Luke 19:14:	Jews from Judea and Jerusalem sent a delegation to Rome to request that someone other than Archelaus govern them.
Luke 19:27:	When Archelaus returned from Rome, he executed the Jews who had gone to Rome to request that someone else govern them. He also killed their families and confiscated their property.

2. Compare Jesus' teaching in Luke 14:31–33 with a widely known fact concerning Herod Antipas:

Details in Jesus' Parable	True Herodian Facts
Luke 14:31–33:	After divorcing his wife, daughter of King Aretas of Nabatea, Herod had to defend himself against the army of Aretas, but he lost badly.

3. As recorded in Matthew 20:25–28, what did Jesus say to His disciples about the politicians of His day?

WORTH OBSERVING

Although Jesus exposed and criticized some of the Pharisees, not all of the Pharisees were hypocrites. Some of them were not far from God's kingdom (Mark 12:34) or had entered it (Acts 15:5). Others supported Jesus and tried to protect Him (John 3:1–2; 7:50–51; Luke 13:31). Jesus never criticized them for being Pharisees, but He criticized their hypocrisy—the fact that they knew the truth but didn't live by it. Jesus commanded His followers to obey the Pharisees (Matthew 23:2–7) but not to imitate their hypocrisy. The apostle Paul remained a Pharisee after becoming a follower of Jesus. (See Acts 23:6; Philippians 3:4–5.)

The Theater

Herod the Great popularized the theater in Israel. The plays often focused on gods and goddesses, mocked honorable and sacred things, and were bawdy and obscene. Featured actors "painted" their faces to portray different characters or emotions, and leading actors were announced with trumpets. The Greek word for "stage actor" was *hypocrite*.

The Jewish community considered theaters to be immoral, and the Talmud taught that no one should attend them. There is no evidence that Jesus participated in or attended the theater, but He clearly was familiar with this aspect of His culture. By speaking its "language," he could communicate to those who knew the theater, including the pagans of the Decapolis.

4. How is each of the following examples related to stage actors, and what is the point of each teaching?

    a. Matthew 6:2–4

Theater at Sepphoris

b. Matthew 6:16–18

c. Matthew 23:23–28

FOR FURTHER STUDY

The book *Roaring Lambs: A Gentle Plan to Radically Change Your World* by Robert Briner (Grand Rapids: Zondervan, 1993) makes a powerful case for learning to speak to a desperate culture in ways it understands. It includes many examples and recommendations.

DATA FILE

The Theaters of Jesus' Day

More than any other person, Herod the Great was responsible for bring-ing the theater to Israel. His campaign to make humanistic Hellenism the worldview of his people included building theaters at Caesarea, Jericho, Jerusalem, Samaria, and Sidon. Many other places including Susita, Sep-phoris, the Decapolis, and Beth Shan had theaters as well. Certainly the first-century theater, which often opposed the God-centered worldview of the Jews, was an important influence.

The splendor and size of Hellenistic theaters, such as the one in Sep-phoris, were seductive and overwhelming to the Jewish people. Imagine the temptation of living in a small village such as Nazareth with a few hundred people and then having the opportunity to see sensual plays in a beautiful theater that could hold thousands of spectators. The religious community, realizing the pull of the theater, resisted it strongly. An ancient rabbi named Yitzak is quoted in the Megilla, a collection of Jew-ish sayings, as believing that Caesarea and Jerusalem could not prosper at the same time. Either one or the other would be in ruins. He clearly understood that the values represented by Caesarea and the theater were antithetical to those of Jerusalem and the temple.

Theater at Caesarea

faith Lesson

Time for Reflection

Read the following passage of Scripture and take the next few minutes to consider the ways in which Jesus communicated to the diverse people of His culture.

> "Be careful not to do your 'acts of righteousness' before men, to be seen by them. If you do, you will have no reward from your Father in heaven.
>
> "So when you give to the needy, do not announce it with trumpets, as the hypocrites do in the synagogues and on the streets, to be honored by men. I tell you the truth, they have received their reward in full. But when you give to the needy, do not let your left hand know what your right hand is doing, so that your giving may be in secret. Then your Father, who sees what is done in secret, will reward you.
>
> "And when you pray, do not be like the hypocrites, for they love to pray standing in the synagogues and on the street corners to be seen by men. I tell you the truth, they have received their reward in full. But when you pray, go into your room, close the door and pray to your Father, who is unseen. Then your Father, who sees what is done in secret, will reward you. And when you pray, do not keep on babbling like pagans, for they think they will be heard because of their many words. Do not be like them, for your Father knows what you need before you ask him."
>
> MATTHEW 6:1–8

1. Note the various cultural images—the "language"—Jesus used in this short portion of Scripture to communicate with His audience.

2. In what ways have you spoken a "language" that is foreign to the secular culture around you when you have tried to communicate the gospel message to others?

3. In what ways are you effectively communicating God's truths to secular culture?

4. Jesus adjusted His teaching to the worldview of His audience without compromising His message. Can you think of a way in which you could tailor your sharing of God's truths to people at work? In your neighborhood? In your family? To children? To someone of a different race or ethnic group?

5. Is it appropriate to communicate the message of Jesus by means that are also used by secular culture? If so, in what way(s) might you be able to use popular music, theater, movies, television, or computer technology to communicate the gospel to people in your culture?

Action Points

Take a moment to review the key points you explored today, then write down an action step (or steps) that you will commit to this week as a result of what you have learned.

1. *We need to discover and understand what shapes our culture.* Jesus participated in the culture of His world and learned its politics, concerns, trends, and passions. He interacted with many different kinds of men, women, and children: powerful leaders and impoverished peasants, religious teachers and lepers, farmers and fishermen, laborers and prostitutes, children of the rich and poor.

   Do you understand what's going on in the worlds of the people you meet—the issues that concern them, the trends that influence them, the passions that drive them, the fears that haunt them?

   What do you need to learn about your world in order to reach people effectively with Jesus' transforming message?

2. *Isolation from culture is not the solution to cultural change.* Jesus understood the culture, language, and people of His day. He knew what would communicate to the people of His world, and He used that knowledge with power. Without modifying or changing God's message, Jesus found ways

to communicate in a "language" of words and ideas that people of His culture spoke and understood. He used the gifts and abilities He had in order to effectively communicate His message of repentance and salvation to everyone He met. In so doing, He made a lasting impact for God.

If we are to reach people with Jesus' transforming message, we also need to work within our culture and communicate through the "language" of ideas and experiences that people in our world understand.

God has given you a unique opportunity to reach people in your world—family members, classmates, neighbors, coworkers, community leaders—with His message. In what ways are you using words and ideas that your culture understands in order to faithfully communicate Jesus' message to people?

What specific things will you do to broaden your understanding of your culture so that you can better communicate Jesus' message to the people of your world?

DATA FILE

The Pharisees

Their History

When the Maccabees opposed the Greeks in 167 B.C., they were supported by a group of pious Jews called the Hasidim. These mighty warriors were devoted to God and sought to obey Him in everything they did. But eventually the Jewish leaders (descendants of the Maccabees) became as Hellenistic as the Greeks, and the devout Jews separated themselves from the Jewish leaders in Jerusalem.

Some of these separatists became Zealots who chose to battle the influence of paganism violently—among their fellow Jews as well as the Romans. Another group of separatists decided that violence would not work. These separatists believed (1) that God had allowed (even caused) the foreign oppression because His people had failed to obey the Torah and (2) that people should devote themselves to completely obeying every detail of law and separating themselves from all influences and people who might interfere with that devotion. These separatists took the name translated "separate" or "separatists" (perushim), which means "Pharisee" in English. Committed totally to God, they assumed the responsibility of leading Israel back to Him. By the time of Jesus, there were more than six thousand Pharisees.

The Pharisees' Beliefs

The Torah was the focus of the Pharisees' lives. They believed that Moses had given a two-part law: the written law of Torah and additional oral commandments that had been passed from generation to generation to help the faithful understand and apply the written law. The Pharisees continued to interpret and expand the Torah to cover every possible occurrence of unfaithfulness to the written law. As you might expect, this oral law became a complex guide to everyday life—far more complicated than most people could understand. In fact, the Pharisees' "yoke" of Torah—the method of obedience—was so difficult to understand that it sometimes obscured the very law they sought to obey.

THE TRUTH OF THE MATTER

Jesus and the Pharisees

Many Pharisees were a powerful force for good among Jesus' people and had a theology similar to the one developed by the early Christians. Many Pharisees supported Jesus' ministry, frequently inviting Him to their homes (Luke 7:36; 14:1) and warning him of Herod's plot (Luke 13:31). Some Pharisees, in fact, accepted Christ (see Acts 15:5) and kept teaching other people (Acts 23:6; Philippians 3:4–6). Note the following beliefs that the Pharisees had in common with Jesus:

- Belief in the physical resurrection of the dead.
- Belief in a coming Judgment Day followed by reward or punishment.
- Expectation of the Messiah's return.
- Belief in angels.
- Recognition of a combination of free choice and divine control in human life.
- Belief that God was all wise, all knowing, just, merciful, and loving.
- Belief in the importance of completely obeying God's law.
- Belief in people's power to choose good or evil, using the Torah as their guide.

Despite these similarities, Jesus did have some conflicts with the Pharisees. Although many Pharisees set high moral standards and tried to remain devoted to God in a hostile world without resorting to the Zealots' violence, some Pharisees were not godly and righteous. Some were so zealous concerning interpretations of oral law that they violated the very letter of the Torah. Other Pharisees focused so much on obedience that they didn't notice or care about people's needs. Unfortunately, history perceives Pharisees as hypocrites and stubborn, uncaring, religious fanatics who rejected and hated Jesus and worked to obtain His arrest and conviction. Jesus, however, understood their thinking and often tailored His message to make sure the Pharisees would understand it.

It is important to realize that Jesus never criticized anyone for *being* a Pharisee. He criticized only hypocritical Pharisees (Matthew 23) and those who spoiled the entire group (Matthew 16:6, 11). Jesus instructed His

(continued on page 170)

(continued from page 169)

disciples to obey what the Pharisees taught (Matthew 23:2–3) but not to practice their hypocrisy.

The Pharisees differed significantly from the Sadducees, another group of religious Jewish leaders with whom Jesus communicated. Notice the contrasts:

Pharisees	Sadducees
Committed to studying and obeying the Torah and oral law	Controlled the economy of the temple in Jerusalem; faithful to temple rituals but often Hellenistic in lifestyle
Had a minor role in the Sanhedrin—the ruling religious council used by the Herods and Romans as the instrument to govern the Jewish people	Had a majority in the Sanhedrin—the ruling religious council
Believed in the Torah and oral law	Believed in the written Torah and rejected oral law; opposed the Pharisees until the temple was destroyed in A.D. 70 (and they ceased to exist); believed study of Torah undermined temple ritual
Believed in bodily resurrection and angels	Didn't believe in bodily resurrection and most Pharisaical doctrine concerning angels and spirits
Gained authority based on piety and knowledge	Gained authority through position and birth
Worshiped in the synagogue	Believed synagogue worship undermined temple ritual and the economy of the temple (their income)
As a whole, were not intimidated by Jesus	Feared and hated Jesus, whose popularity might jeopardize their position in the Sanhedrin and Rome's support

misguided faith

questions to think about

1. What do you think draws people to Jesus?

2. Think about the people who have guided you in your discovery of and walk with God. What about them drew you toward God?

3. What things do Christians in our culture do that tend to turn people away from God rather than toward Him?

video notes

The Crusaders' Fort

The Crusaders' Actions and Motivation

The Damaging Consequences of the Crusaders

Our Response: Choosing Jesus' Message and His Methods

video highlights

Look at the map of the Roman Empire below. Note how far the Crusaders had to travel to get to the Holy Land. Try to imagine the destruction and killing that took place all along their route. It's nearly impossible to comprehend what was done in the name of Jesus, isn't it?

1. What did you think when you saw the European-style Crusader fort high above the Jordan Valley?

2. What stood out to you as you learned about the Crusades?

The Roman World

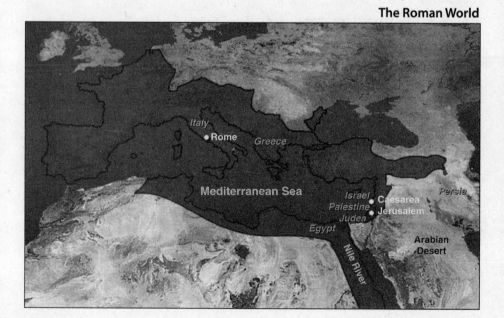

3. What happens to people's view of Christianity when those who are supposed to be imitating Jesus choose their own methods?

4. Do you agree with Ray Vander Laan that it's important not to use language that reminds people of the Crusades? Why or why not?

DATA FILE

The Fortress of Belvoir

Built by the Knights of the Order of the Hospitalers in the twelfth century, this isolated fortress protected the eastern side of the Crusaders' kingdom. Perched on a hill of the Issachar Plateau 1,700 feet above the Jordan Valley, this fortress enabled the Crusaders to control the road below and "protected" its inhabitants from the local population. From their isolated position, the Crusaders were unable to exert any daily influence on the people in the valley below.

Muslims attacked the fortress from A.D. 1180–1184 and then besieged it again in 1187. After resisting sieges for a total of seven years, the 50 knights and 450 soldiers surrendered and left for Europe. The Muslims then destroyed the fortress so it could never be used again.

Today, the ruins of Belvoir stand as a grim monument to the tragedies that occur when people misunderstand Jesus' message and do not live by the truths He taught. Only by living *in* our culture and confronting evil as it presents itself in daily life are we able to influence it positively for Jesus. Jesus called His people to be community builders, not fortress builders. He called his people to confront evil with the weapons of love, forgiveness, and sacrifice.

Physical Details of the Fortress

- A moat encircled the fortress on three sides.
- The entrance was on the east side.
- Towers stood in each corner and in the center of the outer walls so archers could be closer to attackers. A huge tower defended the gate area.
- Small gates led from each tower into the moat, so knights could attack anyone trying to undermine the walls.
- Inside the outer walls (made of basalt) was a smaller fortress consisting of four vaulted, two-story walls and a courtyard. Upper-story rooms were frescoed plaster.
- Cisterns were dug beneath the vaulted rooms.
- A church made of limestone provided a place for worship on the second floor.

Belvoir

PROFILE OF A MOVEMENT

Soldiers of the Cross

On November 27, 1095, in Clermont, France, Pope Urban II called upon all true Christians to free the Holy Land from the Muslim infidels. Christian pilgrims were unable to visit holy sites, including the Church of the Holy Sepulchre—the most sacred of all shrines. That speech sparked a period of violent conflict between the Christian Europeans and the Muslims of the Middle East. Thousands of knights, serfs, peasants, and even a few kings sewed the sign of the cross on the front of their tunics and went to war for Jesus Christ. The Jews, without a country, were caught in between.

The First Crusade

This crusade began in Clermont, France, as knights, farmers, shopkeepers, and fortune seekers headed east through Germany and then south and east to the Holy Land. Determined to avenge Jesus' crucifixion in blood, the leaders of the Crusade massacred many Jews living in wealthy communities in Germany. Many other Jews committed suicide as the knights and unruly mob entered their towns. Tens of thousands of Muslims were also killed. The Crusaders continued to slaughter innocent people, even Orthodox Christians who had the misfortune to dress or look like Muslims.

Finally the Crusaders reached Jerusalem, which they captured on July 15, 1099. A terrible massacre ensued; streets were awash with the blood of innocent civilians. The Jews and Muslims who survived were sold into slavery, and Christianity had earned a reputation that would last for millennia.

The knights built great, European-style castles on high hills, far from roads and sometimes far from water. Soon the castles became places of refuge, escape, and even prisons. Having traveled thousands of miles to

win the Holy Land and the infidels to God's truth, the European con-
querors had no gospel to offer their subjects. They lived in isolation, not
influencing the day-to-day lives of the common people. Jesus would not
have recognized these soldiers who came to spread His kingdom
because they knew so little of the methods He had taught and the way
of sacrifice He had walked.

The Second Crusade

In 1144, an itinerant monk began urging soldiers to destroy the Jewish communities of Germany to avenge Jesus' crucifixion. As a result,
many more innocent people were slaughtered in Jesus' name.

The Third Crusade

Spared the horrors of the first two Crusades, the Jewish communities
in England were not as fortunate during this Crusade in 1170. Jews in
York, Lynn, Norwich, Stamford, and other towns were massacred. Thus
England, too, joined the roster of countries whose Christian armies dis-
tinguished themselves in their brutality against the "infidels."

The Fourth Crusade

In 1198, Pope Innocent III began the Fourth Crusade. He ordered Jews
to wear badges to identify themselves, then ordered them to be killed
to atone for Jesus' death.

The Shepherds' Crusade

The Crusades formally ended in 1291 when the Holy Land was recaptured by the Muslims. But a few years later, European Jews were sub-
jected to yet another Crusade. Nearly forty thousand, mostly teenage
"Crusaders" pillaged, killed, and burned their way across Europe. Some
sources indicate that 150 communities of Jews were exterminated by
these "soldiers of the cross."

small group bible discovery

Topic A: Jesus' Method of Confrontation

Jesus clearly advocated the confrontation of evil. Whereas our human response often is to confront using violence, Jesus confronted evil in different ways. Let's consider His methods of confrontation.

1. In each of the following Scripture passages, what did Jesus confront, and what can we learn from His attitudes and actions?

Scripture	What Did He Confront?	What Can We Learn from His Method?
Mark 5:1–20		
Matthew 15:21–28		
Matthew 16:21–25		

2. When Jesus healed the Canaanite woman's daughter (see Matthew 15:21–28 above), He was in the region of Tyre and Sidon.

a. What was the reputation of that area? (See 1 Kings 16:31; Isaiah 23:17.)

b. Why did Jesus go there? (See Matthew 9:10–13.)

3. In His Sermon on the Mount, Jesus outlined His battle plan for confronting evil.

a. Which characteristics did Jesus call "blessed"? (See Matthew 5:5–10.)

b. What is the purpose of following Jesus' battle plan? (See Matthew 5:13–16.)

c. How are these characteristics and purposes like and unlike the Crusaders' ways of confronting evil? Our ways of confronting evil?

4. What did Jesus say His followers could expect to encounter as they lovingly carried out His commands and shared His message? What encouragement did He offer? (See Matthew 10:17–28.)

FACTS TO CONSIDER

As They Saw It

Many people during Jesus' time offered their own solutions to the problems of the day, as the following reveals:

Who Offered the Solution	What They Recommended	The Method of Jesus
Pharisees	National obedience to the Torah as a life commitment	Demonstrated His commitment to God by His obedience to the Torah
Essenes	Be separate from the world and wait for God to act	Had a similar theology, yet surrounded Himself with people He loved and to whom He ministered
Zealots	Violence is an appropriate means to bring about God's kingdom in Israel; it was a duty to throw off the chains of Roman rule by every means possible	Taught His disciples to love their enemies
Herodians, Sadducees	Preached cooperation with Rome; sought to maintain the status quo; were willing to compromise God's law	Was unwilling to compromise God's law in order to keep an earthly peace

Topic B: God's People Are to Be Involved in Culture

The Crusaders abandoned Jesus' self-sacrificing methods and isolated themselves from culture. They dominated the political scene, yet had little influence on people's daily lives. God, however, calls His people to live on the crossroads of life so that the world may know that He is truly God.

1. What did God, through the prophet Isaiah, reveal about what His people are to do? (See Isaiah 43:12.)

2. Jesus also instructed His disciples to be His witnesses.

   a. What did Jesus command all of His disciples (including us) to do? (See Matthew 28:19–20.)

   b. In what ways are Jesus' disciples to accomplish this? (See Matthew 5:13–16.)

3. Read Matthew 15:29–38 and note the way in which Jesus demonstrated how to be involved in culture.

4. In 1 Peter 2:11–12 what did the apostle Peter urge his readers to do? Contrast this with how the Crusaders lived.

5. The apostle Paul took his involvement in culture very seriously.

   a. In 2 Corinthians 1:12, how did Paul describe his lifestyle?

   b. Read 1 Corinthians 9:19–23 and note the specific ways in which the apostle Paul conducted himself in his culture. Contrast Paul's example with the conduct of the Crusaders, and with your own.

Paul's Conduct	The Crusader's Conduct	My Conduct
Although he was a free man, he was willing to make himself a slave in order to win others to Christ.		
Although he was free from the law, he was willing to come under the law.		

Paul's Conduct	The Crusader's Conduct	My Conduct
Although he would not compromise obedience to Jesus, he was willing to adjust his lifestyle in order to relate to others.		
He was willing to become weak to win the weak.		
He did everything he could to win people to Jesus.		

Topic C: Who Is Responsible for Jesus' Death?

As Jesus' trial progressed, some people in Jerusalem directed fierce anger and hatred toward Him. When Pilate believed Jesus to be innocent, the mob accepted responsibility for Jesus' death and willingly exclaimed, "Let his blood be on us and on our children!" (See Matthew 27:25.) Since then, many Christians, including the Crusaders, have blamed the Jews for killing Jesus. But did God place the blame for Jesus' death on that Jewish mob and their children? Did the mob speak for all Jews?

1. How did many Jewish people respond to Jesus and His teaching? (See Mark 11:18; Luke 20:39; 21:37–38.)

2. What made it difficult for the chief priests and other religious leaders to arrest and kill Jesus? (See Matthew 26:3–5; Luke 19:47–48; 20:19; 22:1–6.)

3. Which people plotted against Jesus and had Him arrested? (See Luke 19:47; John 11:45–53; 18:12–14.)

4. Who actually was responsible for Jesus' ill treatment and execution? (See Matthew 27:11–14, 26; Luke 18:31–33; 23:20–25; John 19:16.)

5. As Jesus was being led away to be crucified, what did people do? (See Luke 23:26–27.)

6. What was Jesus' attitude toward those who crucified Him? (See Luke 23:34.)

7. What did Ezekiel teach about each person's responsibility to God? (See Ezekiel 18:1–4, 19–20, 30.) How does this teaching apply to the Jews, including those who helped to kill Jesus?

8. How did Paul, who knew that some of the Jews had supported Jesus' crucifixion, respond to the Jews? How did he say God responded to the Jews? (See Romans 10:1, 11–13; 11:1–5, 11.)

9. Read the following verses and answer each question:

    a. For what purpose did Jesus die? (See John 1:29.)

b. Who sent Jesus to die for the sins of the world? Ulti-
    mately, who decided that Jesus would give up His life
    as a sacrifice for us? (See John 3:16; 10:14–18.)

Topic D: Jesus Issues the Commands of God's Kingdom

In everything He did, Jesus displayed God's love. He loved us so much
that He came to sacrifice Himself for the sins of the world. Instead of
destroying all the opposition Jesus encountered, God chose to have
His Son change the world with a confrontational love that reached out
to meet people's needs.

Let's look at the instructions Jesus gave His disciples concerning
how to live in their culture. As His disciples, we have the opportunity
to conduct our lives in a way that will reflect Jesus and His gospel to
spiritually blind, hurting people.

1. What command did Jesus give during the Last Supper to all
    who would be His disciples? Why is it important? (See
    John 13:34–35.)

2. Instead of advocating violent, self-serving means such as those the Crusaders used, what did Jesus advocate as His way of changing the world? Write out how you would live out these commands.

Jesus' Commands	Living Them Out in the World
Matthew 5:5–7:	
Matthew 5:8:	
Matthew 5:9:	
Matthew 5:13–16:	
Matthew 5:23–24:	
Matthew 5:38–42:	
Matthew 5:43–48:	
Matthew 6:14–15:	

ϝɑith Lesson

Time for Reflection

Read the following passages of Scripture and take the next few minutes to consider how we can follow the example of Jesus when confronting evil in our culture.

So Judas came to the grove, guiding a detachment of soldiers and some officials from the chief priests and Pharisees. They were carrying torches, lanterns and weapons.

Jesus, knowing all that was going to happen to him, went out and asked them, "Who is it you want?"

"Jesus of Nazareth," they replied.

"I am he," Jesus said. . . .

"If you are looking for me, then let these men go." . . .

Then Simon Peter, who had a sword, drew it and struck the high priest's servant, cutting off his right ear. (The servant's name was Malchus.)

Jesus commanded Peter, "Put your sword away! Shall I not drink the cup the Father has given me?"

JOHN 18:3–5, 8, 10–11

Finally, all of you, live in harmony with one another; be sympathetic, love as brothers, be compassionate and humble. Do not repay evil with evil or insult with insult, but with blessing, because to this you were called so that you may inherit a blessing. For,

"Whoever would love life
and see good days
must keep his tongue from evil
and his lips from deceitful speech.
He must turn from evil and do good;
he must seek peace and pursue it.
For the eyes of the Lord are on the righteous
and his ears are attentive to their prayer,
but the face of the Lord is against those who do evil."

Who is going to harm you if you are eager to do good? But even if you should suffer for what is right, you are blessed. "Do not fear what they fear; do not be frightened." But in your hearts set apart Christ as Lord. Always be prepared to give an answer to everyone who asks you to give the reason for the hope that you have. But do this with gentleness and respect, keeping a clear conscience, so that those who speak maliciously against your good behavior in Christ may be ashamed of their slander. It is better, if it is God's will, to suffer for doing good than for doing evil.

1 PETER 3:8–17

1. These Scripture passages reveal Peter the swordsman in the Garden of Gethsemane, then Peter the apostle and servant of Jesus. Does the Peter in the garden seem like the same person who said to live in harmony and be sympathetic, compassionate, humble, and loving?

   a. What fundamental change had taken place in Peter regarding his method of confronting evil? How is such a change possible?

b. What became Peter's sole motivation?

c. What do these passages say to you personally?

2. As other people observe your actions and attitudes, what do they see of Jesus?

3. When Peter cut off the servant's ear, Jesus said, "Put your sword away," indicating that His way was to follow a different path. To which of your actions would Jesus say, "Put your _____ away"?

Action Points

Take a few moments to review the key points you explored today, then write down an action step (or steps) that you will commit to this week as a result of what you have learned.

1. *When we present Jesus to other people using methods other than those that He used and taught, we send the wrong message and defame Jesus' reputation.* The era of the Crusades is a great tragedy of the Christian faith. The Crusaders slaughtered and plundered Jews, Muslims—even other Christians—in the name of Jesus. The damage done to Jesus' reputation and the walls erected between Christians and people of other faiths remain even to this day.

   Chances are, you will meet someone whose view of Christianity has been affected negatively by tragedies like the Crusades or who has been treated wrongfully by another Christian. What can you do to help such a person see who Jesus truly is?

   If you know such a person, which steps will you take this week in an effort to undo the damage that has been done to Jesus' reputation?

2. *Jesus wants us to confront the power of evil in our culture, but He wants us to do it as He did—not with the sword, but by offering His life.* So it's important for us, as we confront what

is wrong, immoral, and unjust in our society, to do it in a way that models His attitudes and behavior. We must reject attitudes and methods that communicate that Christianity is anything like what the Crusaders demonstrated it to be. If we want others to know God through us, we must present Him as He has revealed Himself to be. If we are to be His disciples, we must become like Him in every way.

Think about the unique opportunities you have to bring Jesus' message to unbelievers through your actions and attitudes. What will you do this week to lovingly communicate His message—even if difficulties may follow?

What are you willing to do to help bridge the gap between yourself and non-Christians? In what way(s) can you be a "community" builder instead of a "fortress" builder in your culture?

What motivations, attitudes, or methods do you use as you confront evil in your culture that are your own rather than those of Jesus? What will you do to change those this week?

A TRAGIC HISTORY

ca. A.D. 27–30	Jesus' ministry
66–73	First Jewish Revolt against Rome
70	Rome destroys Jerusalem
131–135	Second Jewish Revolt
315	Constantine forbids Jews from proselytizing
439	Jews denied right to hold public office and build new synagogues
600	Pope Gregory forbids Jews from eating with Christians
613	Forced baptisms in Spain; Jews who refuse are expelled and their children under age seven are given to Christians
632	Byzantine emperor Heraclius I forces Jews to either be baptized or be killed
1075	Pope Gregory VII prohibits Jews from holding office in Christian countries
1096	First Crusade (Jewish and Muslim communities are slaughtered across Europe, Turkey, and Israel)
1144	Second Crusade (mobs kill Jews throughout Europe)
1170	Third Crusade (Jews are killed throughout Europe)
1198	Pope Innocent III begins Fourth Crusade and orders Jews killed to atone for Jesus' death (Jews had to wear badges)
1291	Crusaders leave Palestine
1320	Shepherds' Crusade (150 communities of Jews are slaughtered in Europe)
1933–45	Nazi Holocaust

HISTORICAL PROFILE

The Jews: A History of Persecution

The New Testament records bitter disagreements over significant beliefs between some Jews (particularly the Sadducees and certain groups of Pharisees) and early Christians. Still, the disciples and apostles continued to try to persuade Jewish people to follow Jesus (Romans 12).

Long after New Testament times, Christians began to blame all Jews for rejecting and crucifying Jesus. Church fathers like Augustine and Justin Martyr taught that the Jews were eternally cursed by God. Soon regular sermons were preached on the Christian holy days of Good Friday and Easter, blaming Jews for Jesus' death. (The fact that Jesus went willingly to His death because of the sins of all people was ignored. Little was said, too, about the Roman soldiers who actually crucified Jesus.)

Constantine, the first Christian emperor, passed many anti-Jewish laws. Popes like Gregory VII forbade interaction between Jews and Christians, and barred Jews from holding office. Jews, in the view of many Christians, were God's enemies. In spite of this oppression, Jewish communities survived and flourished. This increased Gentiles' resentment and led to more abuse of the Jews.

Forced conversions and baptisms of Jews became increasingly common, and local violence occasionally flared, wiping out entire communities. Absurd rumors, such as the accusation that Jews stole Christian children in order to use their blood to make unleavened bread for Passover, ran rampant. Consequently, although not a single example of this has ever been proved, thousands of innocent Jewish people died at the hands of their "Christian" neighbors.

Thus the Crusades simply expanded the violence against Jews to include Muslims as well. Yet, when the Crusades were over, the violence didn't end. Jewish property was routinely seized for hundreds of years. During the Inquisition (from the 1100s through the 1500s), entire communities of Jews were brutally tortured and destroyed, and thousands of others were forced to become Christians. Three hundred thousand Jews were expelled from Spain the year Columbus discovered America. In 1298, more than one hundred thousand Jews were killed in Germany;

two thousand were burned to death in Strasbourg. Martin Luther wrote "Against Jews and Their Lies," a strident treatise condemning Jews to the flames of hell forever. Jewish persecution continued in Russia, Poland, Hungary, and the Ukraine. Still the Jewish communities flourished. Then came the Holocaust . . . .

Only recently have formal steps been taken to renounce this part of Christian history. The Roman Catholic Church's Second Vatican Council affirmed the Jewish roots of Christianity and repudiated collective Jewish guilt for Jesus' death. The Lutheran Church in the United States recently voted to repudiate anti-Semitic teachings of Martin Luther. Many individual Christians have recognized the devastating effects that the Crusades had on non-Christians' views of Jesus and His teaching, and many are rediscovering the Jewish roots of Christianity.

Living Water

Questions to Think About

1. When there is a drought and plants start to turn brown, wither, and die, what happens when water is provided?

2. Suppose you live in a dry region and someone offers you and everyone else in the area all the pure, running water you need if you but ask for it. So you ask every day and receive an abundance of water. But some people won't ask for the water, and some don't seem to know that they have access to an abundant supply. So they struggle to dig up the sunbaked ground in hopes of finding enough water to keep themselves alive. What would your response be to those people?

video notes

Water in the Wilderness—A Spring of Life

The "Living Water" of God

The "Dead Water" of Our Own Cisterns

God as Our Oasis

video нighlights

1. Look at the map below and find En Gedi. Notice how close
    it is to the Dead Sea (about a mile), how isolated it is from
    the civilization of the Judea Mountains, and how expan-
    sive the wilderness is from north to south. The abundant,
    rushing water of this spring would certainly be a relief in
    this part of the wilderness!

2. What did you notice about the oasis of En Gedi?

The Judea Wilderness

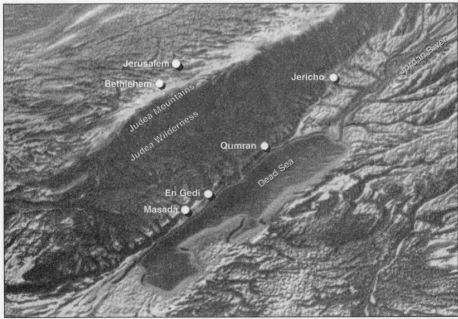

3. How do you think David and his men felt when they took refuge at this oasis?

4. In what ways has your understanding of "living water" and "cistern water" changed as a result of this video?

5. If life is indeed like the wilderness, why is spending time with God each day so important?

DATA FILE

The Oasis of En Gedi

Oasis of En Gedi

Located along the eastern edge of the hot, barren Judea Wilderness where it seldom rains, this oasis is fed by springs. Miles away, in the Judea Mountains, rainfall seeps down into cracks in the rock until it emerges as water gushing from the rock. Just a few hundred yards west of the waterfall shown in the video, water literally streams from a rock.

Many Bible passages speak of water gushing from rock, such as Exodus 17:6; Deuteronomy 8:15; and Psalm 105:41. This adds to our understanding of God and His provision for us. The Bible describes God as the Rock from which water came (1 Corinthians 10:3–4; see also Deuteronomy 32:4, 31; Psalm 78:35).

Ibex

Since En Gedi belonged to the tribe of Judah, it was the place where David hid from King Saul. David and his men no doubt appreciated the cool shade, lush beauty, pools and streams of water, and abundant wildlife of En Gedi after hiding from Saul in the dry wilderness. In this context, David wrote Psalms 42 and 63. Today, desert goats known as ibex graze on the sparse grasses in the desert around En Gedi. They come to the oasis to drink even when people are nearby because they are so thirsty.

small group bible discovery

Topic A: God's Wonderful Gift of Living Water

The springs of En Gedi provide a vivid picture of God as living water.

1. To what did God liken Himself? (See Jeremiah 2:13; 17:13.)

2. To what did David compare his thirst for God? (See Psalm 63:1.)

3. To what did the prophet Jeremiah compare a person who trusts in himself or herself rather than in God? (See Jeremiah 17:5–6.)

4. Read Psalm 78:15–16; Isaiah 41:17–20; 58:11. List the images of living water and an oasis that illustrate what God provides for His people. Notice how similar these images are to the springs of En Gedi.

5. What did Jesus say about the "living water" He came to give? (See John 4:13–14.)

6. At the end of the Sukkot, the Feast of Tabernacles, Jesus offered a bold invitation regarding living water. (See John 7:37–39.)

   a. What did Jesus invite crowds of people to do?

   b. What did Jesus promise to those who did that?

   c. Whom did John say the living water symbolizes?

DATA FILE

The Feast of Sukkot

During Old Testament times, God instituted a religious calendar for the Israelites to follow. The seventh day, the seventh year, and the end of seven "seven years" were significant to Him. Within each year, there were seven specified feasts (Leviticus 23), which included the Feast of Sukkot (or Tabernacles).

The weeklong celebration of Sukkot began after the fall harvest, a time to be especially thankful for God's blessings. Following God's command, the people came to Jerusalem and built booths of olive, palm, and myrtle branches (Nehemiah 8:15), which provided shade. The people were to leave enough space in the branches so that they could see the sky, reminding them of their wilderness years. These booths (*sukkot*, plural: *sukkah*) gave the feast its name.

For seven days, the people ate, lived, and slept in these booths. It was a time to praise God for His past gifts of freedom, land, and bountiful harvests. In fact, God commanded them to "rejoice" before Him (Leviticus 23:40).

A special element of the celebration of Sukkot involved living water. Sukkot took place at the end of the dry season, so the rains needed to begin immediately to ensure a bountiful harvest the following year. Thus the celebration of God's harvest was coupled with the people's fervent prayers for the next year's rains. The priests, too, added a ceremony that included a prayer for rain.

During this ceremony, a procession of priests marched from the temple to the Pool of Siloam, which was fed by the Spring of Gihon. One priest filled a golden pitcher with water, and the procession returned to the temple. At that time, the priest carrying the pitcher stood near the top of the altar and solemnly poured the water into one of two silver funnels leading into the stone altar for the daily drink offerings. At this time, the people—accompanied by the Levitical choir—began a chant that meant, "O Lord, save us by sending rain as well." In this way, they asked God for life-giving rain.

Four great menorahs (more than seventy-five feet high) were also placed in the women's court of the temple. They commemorated the

(continued on page 204)

(continued from page 203)

miraculous burning of a small amount of sacred oil for eight days in the menorah (eternal light) in the Holy of Holies after Judah Maccabee defeated the Greek army of Antiochus and reclaimed Jerusalem.

In the context of Sukkot, the water ceremony, and the menorahs blazing with light, Jesus presented the message of His new kingdom. He had traveled to Jerusalem for Sukkot (John 7:10) and had taught great crowds thronging the temple (John 7:14). On the "last and greatest day of the Feast" (John 7:37), during the water ceremony, the chanted prayers, and the plea made through the offering of living water, Jesus stood and said, "If anyone is thirsty, let him come to me and drink. Whoever believes in me, as the Scripture has said, streams of living water will flow from within him" (John 7:37–38). So, the setting in which Jesus chose to give this lesson, and the similarity of His meaning to Jewish tradition, meant that His shouted promise in the temple must have had stunning impact: "Let him come to *Me!*"

Sukkot is a feast that will be fully realized in heaven. There, God's people will experience living water (Revelation 7:17), His eternal presence (Revelation 21:22), and the light of God (Revelation 22:5). Whereas Sukkot taught the Jewish people to be joyful, in anticipation of heaven, imagine the most joyful celebration that ever existed lasting for eternity. That, indeed, is heaven!

Topic B: Living Water or Broken Cisterns—The Choice Is Ours

Cisterns represent, in one sense, our own efforts and strength. In the language of Scripture, trying to live without God is like turning away from the gushing, cool springs of En Gedi to seek dirty water from broken cisterns.

1. Psalm 107:4–9 describes the condition of the Jews during their desert wanderings and what God did for them.

   a. What was their condition before they turned to God?

   b. After they turned to God—their source of living water—what did He do for them?

A Broken Cistern

2. Before the Israelites entered the Promised Land, what serious warning did God give to His people? (See Deuteronomy 8:10–18.)

Water from Rock

3. In Jeremiah 2:13, we discover what God's people did once they were settled in the Promised Land.

a. Which two sins did God's people commit?

b. What does this verse reveal about our human tendencies?

4. What is the tragedy of turning away from God and depending upon our own cisterns? (See Jeremiah 14:3–4.)

5. In contrast, when a person spends time in God's "oasis"—praying, reading and meditating on the Bible, worshiping, obeying God—instead of trying to dig his or her own cistern, what is he or she compared to in Psalm 1:1–3?

DATA FILE

What Was "Cistern Water"?

An Essene Cistern

In Israel, the rainy season is only five months long, from November through March. Since fresh springs like those at En Gedi are rare, most ancient cities, towns, and even households used cisterns to catch and store runoff from rooftops, courtyards, or even streets. So cistern water wasn't like the clean, fresh, cool, flowing water of a spring. It was likely to be stale and dirty—perhaps even fouled by dead animals.

Furthermore, cisterns were dug by hand out of solid rock and were plastered so they would hold water. They needed constant care because the plaster tended to fall off, which allowed the precious water to leak out. When a cistern failed to hold water, it created a desperate situation for the people who depended on it.

DID YOU KNOW?

Cisterns Were Used for More Than Water!

Served as prisons	(Joseph) Genesis 37:21–28; (Jeremiah) Jeremiah 38:6–13
Symbololized prosperity	2 Kings 18:28–32
Served as hiding places	1 Samuel 13:6
Used as tombs	Jeremiah 41:7–9
Built by kings as well as common people	2 Chronicles 26:9–10
Used in teaching metaphors	Proverbs 5:15–18

Topic C: Living in the Wilderness

As the Jews—God's chosen people—faced the scorching, dry wilderness, God responded to their needs. Using the desert metaphor to describe the struggles of life, and En Gedi with its freshwater springs to describe God's provision, we can say that God still meets the needs of His people in the wilderness of life.

1. How did God provide for the Israelites as they wandered in the wilderness? (See Psalm 105:37–41.)

2. What did God promise to do for the Israelites if they faithfully obeyed His commands, loved Him, and served Him devotedly? (See Deuteronomy 11:10–15.)

3. What does Psalm 107:1, 8–9 reveal about God—and how we should respond to Him?

4. What does God promise to do for the poor and needy? Why? (See Isaiah 41:17–20.)

5. What did Isaiah prophesy concerning the future of God's people and His eternal provision for them? (See Isaiah 35:6–10.)

6. What beautiful image did Jeremiah use to describe a person who trusts in God and His provision? (See Jeremiah 17:7–8.)

7. As God provides for us, what does He expect us to do? (See John 7:38; Mark 9:41.)

Topic D: Our God—An Oasis in the Wilderness

Trusting God for survival means taking the time to come to our "En Gedi" to be refreshed from the rigors of the wilderness of life. The biblical wilderness metaphors used for God communicated powerfully to those who experienced life as wanderers in a danger-filled wilderness. When we see God in this way, and ask Him for help, He will respond with encouragement and comfort.

1. Which imagery did Paul use to describe the Israelites' source of spiritual "living" water that quenched their spiritual thirst? (See 1 Corinthians 10:1–4.)

2. Life in the wilderness is often like being in the brutal heat of the sun. It dries us out, weakens us, and overheats us. In the context of wilderness living, what do the following verses reveal about God as our oasis?

Scripture	God as Our Oasis
Psalm 18:2	
Psalm 61:1–4	
Psalm 91:1–2	
Psalm 121:5–8	
Isaiah 25:4–5	

3. The Word of God helps provide the refreshment and nour-
    ishment we need to survive the wilderness. Which images
    did the psalmist use to describe the Word of God? (See
    Psalm 19:9b–11.)

4. Living in the "wilderness" of culture is not without pur-
    pose. The wilderness is where we learn to depend on God,
    and it is where we are called to be witnesses for Him.

    a. As we live in the "wilderness" of our culture, what does
        God do for us? (See Isaiah 58:11.)

    b. What enables us to keep being effective for God while
        we are in the wilderness? (See Jeremiah 17:5–8.)

5. When God finally establishes His heavenly kingdom, what
    does He promise to do for those who believe in Him? (See
    Isaiah 35:6–7.)

faith lesson

Time for Reflection

Review the words to the song, "En Gedi," and spend a few minutes reflecting on how essential the refreshment of God's living water is in your life.

> Life is not so easy,
> As a Christian standing stone.
> It's a barren wilderness,
> You can't make it on your own.
> For work to be a good thing
> You must face the dusty heat.
> But you're called to find some rest,
> Gaining strength to not be beat.
> Do not dig a cistern,
> Letting pleasures get ahead.
> For the water you need clean,
> Will be stale and dry instead.
> But the waters of En Gedi,
> Are fresh and flow with life.
> So find the Lord in prayer,
> Quench your thirst, and end your strife.
> Oh, En Gedi, taking refuge in the Lord,
> En Gedi, letting Jesus' words reward.
> Drinking living water,
> Resting in the shade.
> Finding all the comfort,
> To never be afraid.
> En Gedi, a quiet peace with God.
>
>   —Ben Lappenga

1. How does living in your culture (the desert wilderness) affect your desire for God (the oasis of En Gedi)?

2. In what ways has God been like the oasis of En Gedi for you? How does that help you face the wilderness of today?

3. Where can you find an "En Gedi," a place where you can become restored with God's shade and living water, in the midst of your busy days?

4. Although it is tempting to stay at En Gedi—the refreshing oasis of God's presence—God calls you to live in a difficult world (the wilderness) so that you can be His witness. How effectively are you reaching out to spiritually thirsty people in the wilderness?

Action Points

Take a few minutes to review the key points you explored today, then write down an action step (or steps) that you will commit to this week as a result of what you have learned.

1. *Just as David and his men needed the life-giving, living water of En Gedi in order to survive their time in the wilderness, God's people today need God's life-giving, living water in order to serve Him in the wilderness of life.*

   When we are nourished and filled with His living water, we will overflow with streams of living water that we can share with thirsty, needy people who live in a spiritually barren world (John 7:38). But in order to have anything to give, we need to have an En Gedi—times of devotion, Bible study, prayer, retreat, meditation—where we can meet with God to satisfy our own spiritual thirst.

   What will you do this coming week to guarantee that you will have time with God—your "oasis" who will give you what you need in order to flourish?

2. *Accept no substitutes for living water! Although many things in our culture may look like living water, they all fail to give us life, to satisfy our thirst for God.* The Dead Sea, for example, looks refreshing from a distance, but its bitter saltwater cannot satisfy. It is equally foolish to turn our backs on God's pure, refreshing, life-giving water and try to dig our own cisterns, which if they hold water at all, can provide only dead, stagnant water.

Which "cisterns" have you built in the past? And which "cisterns" are you building, or are tempted to build, today? Which "Dead Seas" seem inviting to you?

What will you do to seek out God's "living water" this week?

additional Resources

History

Connolly, Peter. *Living in the Time of Jesus of Nazareth.* Tel Aviv: Steimatzky, 1983.

Ward, Kaari. *Jesus and His Times.* New York: Reader's Digest, 1987.

Whiston, William, trans. *The Works of Josephus: Complete and Unabridged.* Peabody, Mass.: Hendrikson Publishers, 1987.

Wood, Leon. Revised by David O'Brien. *A Survey of Israel's History.* Grand Rapids: Zondervan, 1986.

Jewish Roots of Christianity

Stern, David H. *Jewish New Testament Commentary.* Clarksville, Md.: Jewish New Testament Publications, 1992.

Wilson, Marvin R. *Our Father Abraham: Jewish Roots of the Christian Faith.* Grand Rapids: Eerdmans, 1986.

Young, Brad H. *Jesus the Jewish Theologian.* Peabody, Mass.: Hendrickson Publishers, 1995.

Geography

Beitzel, Barry J. *The Moody Atlas of Bible Lands.* Chicago: Moody Press, 1993.

Gardner, Joseph L. *Reader's Digest Atlas of the Bible.* New York: Reader's Digest, 1993.

General Background

Alexander, David, and Pat Alexander, eds. *Eerdmans' Handbook to the Bible.* Grand Rapids: Eerdmans, 1983.

Butler, Trent C., ed. *Holman Bible Dictionary.* Nashville: Holman Bible Publishers, 1991.

Edersheim, Alfred. *The Life and Times of Jesus the Messiah.* Peabody, Mass.: Hendrickson Publishers, 1994.

Archaeological Background

Charlesworth, James H. *Jesus Within Judaism: New Light from Exciting Archaeological Discoveries.* New York: Doubleday, 1988.

Finegan, Jack. *The Archaeology of the New Testament: The Life of Jesus and the Beginning of the Early Church.* Princeton: Princeton University Press, 1978.

Mazar, Amihai. *Archaeology of the Land of the Bible: 10,000–586 B.C.E.* New York: Doubleday, 1990.

To learn more about the specific backgrounds of this set of videos, consult the following resources:

Avigad, Nahman. "Jerusalem in Flames—The Burnt House Captures a Moment in Time." *Biblical Archaeology Review* (November-December 1983).

Barkey, Gabriel. "The Garden Tomb—Was Jesus Buried Here?" *Biblical Archaeology Review* (March-April 1986).

Ben Dov, Meir. "Herod's Mighty Temple Mount." *Biblical Archaeology Review* (November-December 1986).

Bivin, David. "The Miraculous Catch." *Jerusalem Perspective* (March-April 1992).

Burrell, Barbara, Kathryn Gleason, and Ehud Netzer. "Uncovering Herod's Seaside Palace." *Biblical Archaeology Review* (May-June 1993).

Edersheim, Alfred. *The Temple*. London: James Clarke & Co., 1959.

Edwards, William D., Wesley J. Gabel, and Floyd E. Hosmer. "On the Physical Death of Jesus Christ." *Journal of American Medical Association (JAMA)* (March 21, 1986).

Flusser, David. "To Bury Caiaphas, Not to Praise Him." *Jerusalem Perspective* (July-October 1991).

Greenhut, Zvi. "Burial Cave of the Caiaphas Family." *Biblical Archaeology Review* (September-October 1992).

Hareuveni, Nogah. *Nature in Our Biblical Heritage*. Kiryat Ono, Israel: Neot Kedumim, Ltd., 1980.

Hepper, F. Nigel. *Baker Encyclopedia of Bible Plants: Flowers and Trees, Fruits and Vegetables, Ecology*. Ed. by J. Gordon Melton. Grand Rapids: Baker, 1993.

"The 'High Priest' of the Jewish Quarter." *Biblical Archaeology Review* (May-June 1992).

Hirschfeld, Yizhar, and Giora Solar. "Sumptuous Roman Baths Uncovered Near Sea of Galilee." *Biblical Archaeology Review* (November-December 1984).

Hohlfelder, Robert L. "Caesarea Maritima: Herod the Great's City on the Sea." *National Geographic* (February 1987).

Holum, Kenneth G. *King Herod's Dream: Caesarea on the Sea*. New York: W. W. Norton, 1988.

Mazar, Benjamin. "Excavations Near Temple Mount Reveal Splendors of Herodian Jerusalem." *Biblical Archaeology Review* (July-August 1980).

Nun, Mendel. *Ancient Stone Anchors and Net Sinkers from the Sea of Galilee*. Israel: Kibbutz Ein Gev, 1993. (Also available from *Jerusalem Perspective*.)

_____. "Fish, Storms, and a Boat." *Jerusalem Perspective* (March-April 1990).

_____. "The Kingdom of Heaven Is Like a Seine." *Jerusalem Perspective* (November-December 1989).

_____. "Net Upon the Waters: Fish and Fishermen in Jesus' Time." *Biblical Archaeology Review* (November-December 1993).

_____. *The Sea of Galilee and Its Fishermen in the New Testament*. Israel: Kibbutz Ein Gev, 1993. (Also available from *Jerusalem Perspective*.)

Pileggi, David. "A Life on the Kinneret." *Jerusalem Perspective* (November-December 1989).

Pixner, Bargil. *With Jesus Through Galilee According to the Fifth Gospel.* Rosh Pina, Israel: Corazin Publishing, 1992.

Pope, Marvin, H. "Hosanna: What It Really Means." *Bible Review* (April 1988).

Riech, Ronny. "Ossuary Inscriptions from the Caiaphas Tomb." *Jerusalem Perspective* (July-October 1991).

_____. "Six Stone Water Jars." *Jerusalem Perspective* (July-September 1995).

Ritmeyer, Kathleen. "A Pilgrim's Journey." *Biblical Archaeology Review* (November-December 1989).

Ritmeyer, Kathleen, and Leen Ritmeyer. "Reconstructing Herod's Temple Mount in Jerusalem." *Biblical Archaeology Review* (November-December 1989).

_____. "Reconstructing the Triple Gate." *Biblical Archaeology Review* (November-December 1989).

Ritmeyer, Leen. "The Ark of the Covenant: Where It Stood in Solomon's Temple." *Biblical Archaeology Review* (January-February 1996).

_____. "Quarrying and Transporting Stones for Herod's Temple Mount." *Biblical Archaeology Review* (November-December 1989).

Ritmeyer, Leen, and Kathleen Ritmeyer. "Akeldama: Potter's Field of High Priest's Tomb." *Biblical Archaeology Review* (November-December 1994).

Sarna, Nahum M. *The JPS Torah Commentary: Exodus.* New York: Jewish Publication Society, 1991.

"Sea of Galilee Museum Opens Its Doors." *Jerusalem Perspective* (July-September 1995).

Shanks, Hershel. "Excavating in the Shadow of the Temple Mount." *Biblical Archaeology Review* (November-December 1986).

"Shavuot." *Encyclopedia Judaica,* Volume 14. Jerusalem: Keter Publishing House, 1980.

Stern, David. *Jewish New Testament Commentary.* Clarksville, Md.: Jewish New Testament Publications, 1992.

Taylor, Joan E. "The Garden of Gethsemane." *Biblical Archaeology Review* (July-August 1995).

Tzaferis, Vassilios. "Crucifixion—The Archaeological Evidence." *Biblical Archaeology Review* (January-February 1985).

_____. "A Pilgrimage to the Site of the Swine Miracle." *Biblical Archaeology Review* (March-April 1989).

_____. "Susita." *Biblical Archaeology Review* (September-October 1990).

Vann, Lindley. "Herod's Harbor Construction Recovered Underwater." *Biblical Archaeology Review* (May-June 1983).

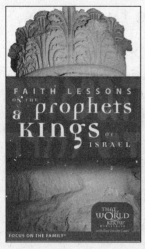
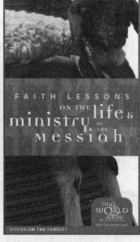
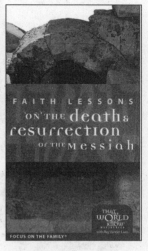

Travel back in time to see the sights, hear the sounds, and experience the wonder of Jesus—all through the power of interactive CD-ROM.

Jesus
An Interactive Journey

Imagine traveling back in time for a life-changing encounter with Christ . . . meeting the people who knew Him . . . retracing His footsteps . . . seeing first-hand what His life was like.

Now, through the cutting-edge technology of interactive CD-ROM, you can make that incredible voyage—back to the life and times of Jesus! This exciting multimedia adventure takes you there, giving you an entirely new appreciation for the fascinating historical, geographical, and cultural backdrop that will enhance your understanding of the Gospel.

An innovative "Visitor's Center" is your gateway to more than 180 different avenues of study, from Christ's birth to His resurrection. With a click of the mouse, you'll be guided to dozens of colorful locales, where you'll experience through the eyes and ears of ancient Jews and Romans what Christ's world was really like.

Or take a self-guided tour and stroll at your own pace through the lively marketplace to learn about trade and commerce, pause to listen in on the people, or go to the synagogue to gain a better understanding of the religious practices of the day.

The high technology and vast amount of material in this unique presentation will captivate you for hours, while providing a solid understanding of the Gospel and its relevance to today's believer. It's great for personal and family Bible study, Christian schools, and a wide variety of church uses.

Compatible with Windows® 95 and Windows® 3.1

CD-ROM   0-310-67888-9

DO YOU REMEMBER WHEN YOU FIRST MET HIM?

Echoes of His Presence

Ray Vander Laan
with Judith Markham

You are taken on an inspirational pilgimage beside the springs of En Gedi, into the Judean mountains, behind the walls of Jerusalem, and into the life of Christ. You'll experience the anticipation of the expectant Jewish culture, a people eager for the coming Messiah, and bask in the wonder of His compassionate ways. And you'll witness the confusion of Jesus' last days on earth, the Savior they had longed for . . . the One they didn't want.

Through historically accurate, fictional stories of people Jesus touched, *Echoes of His Presence* spans the gap between the history of Jewish tradition and the nature of Western thinking, making the Savior's ministry relevant, significant, and more meainful than ever to today's believrs. You'll undestand Scirpture in its cultural context . . . and you'll fall in love with Jesus all over again.

Hardcover 0-310-67886-2
Audio 0-310-67887-0

ZONDERVAN™

GRAND RAPIDS, MICHIGAN 49530
w w w . z o n d e r v a n . c o m

We want to hear from you. Please send your comments about this
book to us in care of the address below. Thank you.

ZONDERVAN™

GRAND RAPIDS, MICHIGAN 49530

www.zondervan.com